Feminist Literary History

For James

Feminist Literary History

A Defence

JANET TODD

Polity Press

First published 1988 by Polity Press
in association with Blackwell Publishers Ltd

Reprinted 1991, 1995

Editorial office:
Polity Press, 65 Bridge Street,
Cambridge CB2 1UR, UK

Marketing and production:
Blackwell Publishers Ltd
108 Cowley Road, Oxford OX4 1JF, UK

ISBN 0-7456-0513-3
ISBN 0-7456-0514-1 (pbk)

A CIP catalogue record for this book is available from the British Library.

Typeset in 10 on 12 pt Baskerville
by Opus, Oxford.
Printed and bound in Great Britain
by Athenæum Press Ltd, Gateshead, Tyne & Wear

Contents

Acknowledgements viii

Introduction 1

1 Early Work 17

2 Consolidation and Reaction 34

3 French theory 51

4 Confrontations 69

5 Directions 85

6 Readings of Mary Wollstonecraft 103

7 Men in Feminist Criticism 118

Conclusion 135

Notes 140

Bibliography 148

Index 157

Acknowledgements

I am grateful to Steve Watts, Naomi Segal, John Mullan, Alice Jardine, Peter Collier, Lisa Jardine and especially Alison Hennegan, for supplying books and articles. I am also grateful to the speakers in the series on feminism and psychoanalysis in Cambridge 1986–7 who were generous with references and who helped me clarify my ideas despite my basic disagreement with their approach. I should like to thank Marilyn Butler and James Lynn for their help and encouragement.

Introduction

It has become fashionable to criticize, even mock, American socio-historical feminist criticism and to see it as naïve beside the enterprise of French deconstructive and psychoanalytical theory. Francophile critics like Toril Moi, Mary Jacobus, and Alice Jardine are exasperated at what they see as benighted empiricism and 'essentialist simplicities'.

Some of the mockery undoubtedly sticks but some should be deflected, deriving as it does from a determined misreading of the method of historical enquiry and a refusal to acknowledge the context in which this criticism was produced. It is easy in the late 1980s to lay out the past in clear space for observation and comparison and ignore the obscured and shifting time in which it occurred. The early socio-historical criticism that is now denigrated formed the base and condition of later study, was in a way the begetter of us all, and so inevitably, like a mother, appears naïve in the light of changing modes. This criticism belonged to a time that still hoped for a wide, increasingly feminist audience; it was written in a more activist and interventionist spirit than seems possible today. The more sophisticated readings that are now privileged derive from a time or a place when certain forms of feminist or gender criticism are inevitably the preserve of the mandarin or the theoretical academic. In the late 1980s women often come into feminist criticism without the apprenticeship or context of active feminism; they may enter it having already established security of tenure through other work or they may arrive through theory rather than protest, through psychoanalysis and deconstruction rather than demonstrations. They may use the distinguishing term 'intellectual' – a term hardly heard in the early 1970s – to describe themselves and their separation from other women.

I should like here to provide not another introduction to feminist criticism – many admirably clear ones are now available – but a defence of the early socio-historical enterprise, together with an assessment of its likely developments and my hopes for a feminist literary history founded on its base. In this enterprise I am no doubt partially motivated by piety – a residue of the filial piety imposed on writing women from the eighteenth century onwards. But I do not believe we must be oedipal, especially not across gender lines.

Yet, while my position is defensive and, ultimately, admiring, I also find much that is limited in this criticism. Elaine Showalter has argued that pioneering socio-historical criticism was not as naïve as it is made out to be, that American feminist criticism in general is 'as theoretically sophisticated as its continental sister'.[1] Perhaps, but I am unconvinced. Instead of arguing for parity, I think it useful to set the early writing within the history of feminist criticism and relate it to a moment when women critics wished to avoid being reliant on abstract systems of thought that could not be appreciated by the philosophically uneducated. It is then possible to accept that initially this criticism was indeed insufficiently aware of the constructed nature of gender identities and the difficulty of self-consciously encountering all our rooted assumptions. It is also possible to admit that it often settled for easy socio-cultural generalizations instead of pursuing the more intractable and specific history.

But with all its faults American socio-historical feminist criticism was pioneering and remains inspirational. Although, in these harsher academic times, most of us have become a little more elitist, it does not follow that we should show embarrassment at the eclecticism and breadth of the earlier work or its insistence that the ultimate aim of feminist criticism should be the subversion of patriarchy, that rule of the fathers that Kate Millett so resoundingly denounced in *Sexual Politics* (1970). It is not necessary to abandon the political context of the earliest works to write criticism today or to praise mental revolution or reform at the expense of the physical and material sort which the founding texts wished to promote. Feminist criticism may have moved into more sophisticated modes but not because its simplest goals of academic and institutional acceptance have been fulfilled. They have not. Men have had power in history and hermeneutics and they still have it, especially in Britain. The arrival of a few women in academic high places has no more transformed the establishment of culture – not to mention the material condition of women's lives – than the arrival of the odd prime minister in Number 10 has transformed the social establishment.

There are some peculiar notions about. One is that feminist criticism has done its work and that the feminist perspective dominates in certain American universities. There has certainly been considerable success but I am not sure that I could locate these exemplary institutions. Yale boasts Barbara Johnson, Shoshana Felman amd Margaret Homans, while Princeton has Elaine Showalter, Sandra Gilbert and Margaret Doody. But neither could be described as a feminist establishment and I do not believe that feminist criticism has yet concluded even the simplest reformist work in institutions.

Another widespread but, I think, equally dubious notion is that a few feminist critics, like Elaine Showalter and Sandra Gilbert, have become wielders of immense academic power, forming a kind of mafia in feminist criticism. Such women have indeed turned into star performers, appearing on academic platforms throughout the United States. But there seems little danger of an improper hegemony; authority of any sort was deeply and constantly questioned at the inception of feminist criticism and is still being questioned at least by those writers within the socio-historical tradition (francophile theoretical critics have a rather different attitude and sometimes appear dazzled by the overpowering and systematic intellectual). If there is any tendency in the authoritarian direction, it is surely mitigated by the eclectic nature of American feminist criticism nowadays when it is taken as a whole and by the appearance of many younger feminist critics who are unlikely to allow in their elders the security and complacency which such academic authority seems to require.

A final notion that I think needs to be countered is the idea that feminist criticism is promoting a separatism that might well have been good in its time but which is now entirely outdated. The recent *Norton Anthology of Literature by Women*, for example, aroused considerable uneasiness in those who regarded it as improper segregation. If this is the prevailing attitude, perhaps feminist critics should point out segregation in other works by providing them with accurate labelling. So *The Oxford Anthology of English Literature: The Restoration and the Eighteenth Century* (1973) could be called the 'Oxford book of male writers' and those many selections of early nineteenth-century poetry could become 'Men Romantics'.

For many feminist critics in the USA, especially those working from within departments of modern languages, one way of avoiding the appearance of segregation – and of naïvety – has been through an attention to the seductive intellectual tones of psychoanalysis, mediated through the French Freudian revisionist Jacques Lacan and the French feminist theoreticians. This approach has replaced history with psychoanalysis and women writers with a mode called 'feminine writing' which can be produced by either sex. The gender of the author becomes a matter of indifference; consequently there can be no fear of separatism and in this sort of criticism the woman writer has about the same amount of attention as she received within traditional critical analysis.

In my concern for socio-historical criticism I will have to say something of this psychoanalytical enterprise since it has both influenced and enraged the critics on whom I am primarily concentrating. I will provide a brief summary for those unacquainted with its assumptions; I will not, however, be concerned to present it impartially – psychoanalytical critics would in any case mock such a project – but accept my own desire to oppose its overwhelming influence and appropriate some of its insights. I will also mention in passing the British tradition of Marxist feminism that has, more recently, impinged on the American consciousness.

But my concern remains primarily with the socio-historical criticism which, with all its limitations, has held resolutely to its rooted conviction that the subject is women, not the human or the humanist condition in general, not 'Woman', not a part of women like the vagina or the uterus nor an expression of women like sexuality or 'feminine writing'. This criticism has been of female experience, then, not some modality that could be subsumed into 'gender studies' or replaced at the proper time by an investigation of masculinity, not something that could be used by successful academic women looking to give an exciting edge to their predominantly male critical theory or by successful academic men metonymically reducing women to a controllable and plastic voice.

The project

I hope briefly to indicate the historical development of this criticism, its reaction to and discomfort with French psychoanalytical and deconstructionist theory, and its most recent developments towards synthesis or specific historical study. For definition I will follow Patricia Spacks, one of its earliest proponents, who took feminist criticism 'to include any mode that approaches a text with primary concern for the nature of female experience in it – the fictional experience of characters, the deducible or imaginable experience of an author, the experience implicit in language or structure'.[2] I will start with the early days in the 1970s, often concentrating on Elaine Showalter who, as a supremely reactive writer, I will use as representative of the various changes and modifications in this criticism. By doing so I am aware that I am omitting many other lines of development, especially those of black and lesbian critics whose work is at the moment among the richest and most provocative in the socio-historical mode, but which in the early years tended to exist in the space provided by the more popular mainline critics. For my account I will inevitably have to distort history to some extent. Although the French psychoanalytical theory was flourishing by the 1970s, its full force was not felt in the USA until the 1980s, except in departments of French; I will therefore discuss the feminist criticism from what Jane Gallop has called 'the exotic space of France' after I have outlined the American position, concentrating less on the theory itself than on its reception by American critics. Consequently, as I have indicated, my concern is not with this criticism in any comprehensive and subtle way but mainly with those few texts that were widely received in the monolingual USA because they were translated, no doubt losing thereby some of their French resonance and mystique.

Alice Jardine, a French-inspired American critic, has recently lamented the prevalent annoyance at theoretical French-based criticism in some academic quarters; it seems to me that American feminist analysis of the socio-historical kind has suffered more completely, partly through direct criticism of its methodology, partly through the condescending assumption that its time in the sun is long past, and partly by a refusal to use on it its own preferred method of historical placing. Yet it has of necessity moved, grown and incorporated as it has travelled through time; it is not a synchronic phenomenon although many of its critics tend to treat it as such. I will try, then, to give an appearance of progress – or rather of movement since I do not hold a Whiggish view of its development – through the years; no doubt there will be much falsification through condensing, displacing and eliminating, but at least I hope a sense of moving might be conveyed.

The confrontation of the two modes, the socio-historical American and the French psychoanalytical, is an exciting spectator sport, but the fight is not over. It is an inevitable contest and should not be avoided; American historical criticism has learnt immeasurably from its antagonist and will no doubt go on learning. But I think too that we should remain in contest and not rush towards some limiting and limited synthesis. I want, then, to stress the great and sometimes beneficial influence of psychoanalytical criticism on the mainline American socio-historical enterprise with its British offshoots, but I do not want to take its direction. For it is, I believe, time to reverse the situation of dominance, to turn history onto psychoanalysis, to historicize its discourse, methods and aims and to contextualize its functioning in the history that it likes to allegorize and abstract, in short to show its implausibility in history but its plausibility as history.

In a highly controversial paper given at the Southampton Sexual Difference Conference in 1985, entitled '"Girl Talk" (for Boys on the Left), or Marginalising Feminist Critical Praxis', Lisa Jardine, a lecturer at Cambridge University, made the necessary point that English was established as an academic subject in Britain as women entered the academy, that literary studies have always risked being dubbed a woman's subject and that the majority of English and modern languages students are female. But the politically progressive men who teach the subjects – women are of course not the majority of lecturers and professors – make little of this sexual identification but tend to achieve authority by transmuting vernacular literary studies into theory and into male-dominated disciplines like social and political science. (One could add psychoanalysis to this.) Lisa Jardine caused an uproar by mentioning that in Cambridge she worked with several 'fascist gay men'. Like the paper itself, the remark, which was later temperately translated as 'fascists who are also homosexual' by Jonathan Dollimore, pointed to problems of power among male and female critics, of feminist studies and gender studies, masculinity and femininity, of appropriation and silencing, that arouse deep emotions.[3] My concern here is not with wider gender studies or with studies of homosexual writing or of masculinity, nor indeed with the tendency to herd literary works into more scientific disciplines, but I do want briefly to look at the impact of all of these on a feminist criticism sometimes made to seem heterosexist and insecure.

Finally I will return to my main subject, the subject of women in history, women who wrote in history and who, ideologically marked and muzzled no doubt, nevertheless wrote with a voice that has never been sufficiently attended to. I should like to urge a kind of historically specific, archival, ideologically aware but still empirically based enterprise, using a sense of specific genre as well as notions of changing female experience. This kind of feminist literary history, calling on the work of British feminists concerned with ideology and on historians of culture, would, I think, be a corrective to the early American feminist criticism, on which it is none the less based but which in its enthusiasm for cultural change rushed into premature and erroneous generalizations. But it would as well be in opposition in its initial modesty to the theoretical modes that have killed off not only the authoritarian male author but the tentative and hardly heard female one as well and have set the 'signifying and dispersed subject' in place of women, ignoring the fact that our notions now are as constructed and historically based as any outdated simplicities of humanism.

Autobiography and the margins of self-indulgence

In view of my desire to place or lightly contextualize feminist criticism, I should perhaps lay out my own trajectory and also give an idea of the difference between academic feminist criticism in the USA where I have worked and Britain where I am writing. By this autobiographical intervention I will be exposing my membership of the older generation of feminists like Kate Millett who, after apologizing for her lack of good taste, transgressed the code of criticism and published her personal experiences. Perhaps inevitably, the enthusiasm and loquacious frankness of my generation have been somewhat embarrassing to younger feminists. Yet it seems to me that one of the strengths of feminist criticism has been its welcoming of the personal, however crude, naïve and untheorized it may sometimes appear and however problematic and constructed the self can be assumed to be. It still remains a refreshing emphasis that the reader is a subject herself and that she does not spend all her time reading.

But of course there is a hidden purpose in this seemingly masochistic self-revelation, a purpose that appears pretty common from my reading of feminist critics. For, by exposing my academic trajectory, I am laying claim to a desirable marginality. No longer officially a 'resident alien' in the USA, that wonderfully comforting identity for the metaphysically insecure, but also no longer a secure and tenured professor of English, I am locating myself outside professional departments and outside the organs of literary power, and using these exclusions as stigmata. Julia Kristeva, the most commanding of the French theoreticians, has famously shown the way by insisting, despite her institutional power and international fame, on her distinguishing Bulgarian background and her location in a foreign language – French. Gayatri Spivak, a well-placed and esteemed academic in the USA, insists on her Third World status. The Scandinavian critic Toril Moi is attracted to the marginal posture as another alien in English-speaking countries; so are the American francophile critics Alice Jardine and Jane Gallop. The last is the most self-conscious of the posture, admiring the 'marginality' of Kristeva and yet commenting, 'how vulgar to flaunt it'; like Alice Jardine, she tries to present an interpretation of her position at home in the USA as one of alienation, anxiously seeking her 'own claim to "dissidence", to being "a new kind of intellectual", to "exile"'.[4]

So there is some complacency in my insistence on my cultural and institutional marginality. The position has a long and honourable history, a fact recently stressed by Roland Barthes who made the margin into the productive space and gave it to the lover, the individual and the self-aware. And no doubt we are all to some extent playing the game that a male writer on feminism, K. K. Ruthven, has described: exaggerating our difficulties 'in order to develop in one another a sense of heroic solidarity in the face of overwhelming odds'[5].

To keep some decent reticence I will present my critical progress as mediated through the public pages of *The Times Literary Supplement* and I will apologize no further for the intrusion, since, as Patricia Spacks has remarked, one cannot, as a feminist critic, afford to sound too tentative in print.

Raised largely in Britain I went to the United States in 1968 with a rare sense of timing. Betty Friedan and Kate Millett were immediate revelations, or perhaps it is truer to say that they articulated what I had incoherently felt; the incoherence was a failure indeed, but it had been much aided by a Cambridge education in the early 1960s under the dominance of F. R. and Q. D. Leavis. While the serious moralistic Leavisite notion of literature had certain attractions over the Oxford Lord David Cecil view of it as both expensive and useless, the emphasis on arrogant disinterestedness, the concern to exclude writers from study and improper readers from studying, and, above all, the absolute refusal to consider its own value-laden concepts and its specific class and gender perspective made it extremely difficult even to express uneasiness in any positive way that might tend to the formulating of an alternative.

In the States I began work in the area of empirical criticism, editing a journal, *Women & Literature*, excavating early women writers like Mary Wollstonecraft and Helen Maria Williams and flirting at the given time with the French methods that were then bombarding the States. This resulted in *Women's Friendship in Literature* concerning eighteenth-century fiction from Richardson and Rousseau to Austen and Sade, and concentrating on the conventions of female relationships especially in epistolary fiction that usually demanded two writing women. The book was well received in the States in 1980 and consequently reissued in paperback in 1984.

Working by now at Douglass College of Rutgers University, I had at one time or another such colleagues as Elaine Showalter, Adrienne Rich, Domna Stanton, and Catherine Stimpson. Nina Auerbach, Nancy Miller, Patricia Spacks, Carolyn Heilbrun and Ellen Moers were more or less down the road. I mention these critics not to inflate myself with their company, but simply to suggest that I might be forgiven for thinking for a while that feminist criticism, riven with contradictions as it was, various in its modes and aims, had in large measure arrived in the academic world. I felt able then to spend a great deal of time compiling an encyclopaedia of women writers of the period which interests me most, the eighteenth century. I hoped that *A Dictonary of British and American Women Writers 1660–1800* which made a beginning in a largely uncharted area would be helpful to students who had been taught that there were no women writers before Jane Austen; indeed many women have written to say that they have found it so. There were some errors in the work which are being collectively eliminated, but, like the earlier book, it was mostly well received especially by journals in the USA concerned with the period under scrutiny.

A Guggenheim Fellowship allowed me to make a return to Britain where I decided to stay. I began work on a book that was intended to contribute to the enterprise of writing women back into literary history. It concerned the movement of sensibility in the eighteenth century taking place in what has been labelled the swamps between the twin peaks of Augustanism and Romanticism. In *Sensibility* I argued that the downgrading of sentimental writing was partly due to its connection with the rise of the woman reader and writer and with the notion of writing of this sort as feminine, so that the reaction when it came in the later eighteenth century was often presented in terms of a new manliness, a resurgence of masculinity and of men speaking to men. I thought of the work as introductory, appropriately so since there existed no book that simply explained the movement or which accounted for the gendered vocabulary used to describe it. Again reviewers in the States were pleasant enough, even generous with their praise.

All this is by way of preamble to the intervention of *The Times literary Supplement*. The books I wrote were each reviewed by this powerful British literary organ and here is what it said. (Ritual debasement in prefaces by women has been a female mode from the eighteenth century onwards but I want to quote mainly to suggest the situation in Britain of feminist criticism and to show that the very fact that one is writing as a feminist is enough to provoke abuse without any attention needed for the specific critical argument presented.)

To begin with *Women's Friendship in Literature*, reviewed by Anita Brookner, later the winner of the Booker Prize for her novel *Hotel du Lac*. Under the title 'Bonding against the Patriarchs' (*TLS*, 20 June 1980, p. 716), she took extreme issue with my book mainly for what it seemed to imply outside itself, a distasteful liking for women verging on the inappropriate. She placed the work on 'the main platform of the more extreme wing of the Women's Movement' and labelled it 'propaganda in favour of the supportive role of women'. While obviously disliking the enterprise, she disliked even more the content of the novels; quoting the famous rapist in Richardson's *Clarissa*, she asserted: 'The tropical heat of female friendships in the eighteenth-century novel was seen even at the time as dangerous, "too vehement to endure," says Lovelace.' Anna Howe, Clarissa's main female correspondent and supporter, became 'no less hungry' for the heroine than the man who raped her, while Claire in Rousseau's *La Nouvelle Héloïse* was an hysteric, a 'frenetic version of Anna Howe'. Both female friends were abused by Brookner because they served to postpone good heterosexual pleasure. In place of the unwholesome books of Richardson and Rousseau, the reviewer urged the period's most famous work of pornography, *Fanny Hill*, because Fanny's well-chosen female friends show her how to please men and 'eclipse themselves discreetly when she achieves the happy marriage that ends the book. Fanny Hill is the only exemplary heroine in the literature of the eighteenth century.'

In the end, though, Brookner switched from the unsavoury fiction of the eighteenth century altogether and put in its place the decent fairy story:

> Let it not be forgotten that in certain myths and legends the function of the hero (the 'prince') was once to deliver the heroine from her female oppressors: Cinderella from her sisters, Snow-White from her stepmother. It is still legitimate to expect this natural progression and to respect it. Any deviation from this line of growth should be narrowly examined for something less or more than 'female bending' [sic].

Fortunately for my credibility (and, it seems, my heterosexuality) I provided some 'exceedingly clever chapters on Jane Austen' which confounded my thesis by showing that heroines indeed cannot have real friends because these might hinder the march towards suitable marriage.

The *Dictionary of British and American Women Writers 1660–1800* fared even worse than *Women's Friendship* in that it received only a paragraph at the end of Brigid Brophy's review of several feminist works (*TLS*, 26 July 1985). Brophy was already known for her acerbic anti-feminism; she had, for example, aimed to demolish Casey Miller and Kate Smith's *Handbook of Non-Sexist Writing* (1982), the result, she assured her readers of a 'leaden literalness of mind' and 'tin ears'; Brophy enjoyed her wit and reprinted the piece in her *Baroque 'N' Roll* (Hamish Hamilton, 1987).

The main brunt of Brophy's *TLS* attack was borne by a very modest work, a reprinting of Renaissance pamphlets on the women's question edited by Simon Shepherd, whose reasonable point about his awareness that he was a male critic working on what women had made was described by Brophy as 'steering pretty directly towards *Private Eye*'s dump for "loony feminist nonsense"'. By the time she reached the *Dictionary* she was sailing at full steam. While searching for Jane Austen who, the preface had clearly explained, was omitted because she was publishing after the end date of the book, she ignored every one of the other 500 or so women writers mentioned, and the entire purpose of the enterprise, to reveal the immense riches of female writing *before* Jane Austen, was lost for her. But, then, why should Brophy attend to the purpose for, by definition, the book was 'offensive to egalitarians' suggesting apartheid and segregation and should not have been written? Such works were on a par with children's books and cookery manuals and no real buyer would want them: 'Feminism may lack allure for individual book-buyers, but the posse of jackboot feminists can no doubt be counted on to bully institutions.'[6]

Finally *Sensibility*, reviewed by *TLS* on 27 February, 1987, by an American male academic, W. B. Carnochan. Again not a word about the object of the book, the writing of women back into cultural history, but simply abuse. I was, the California professor reiterated, making 'rice pudding' rather than rice. This argument through trope was undoubtedly intended to be rude but the precise meaning remained obscure. Perhaps it harked back to Dr. Johnson's belittling praise of the good puddings of Elizabeth Carter, famous translater of Epictetus, or perhaps it implied that men made rice – rather a blasphemous though not untypical assertion. Certainly Carnochan was having no truck with my women writers, who were not mentioned in his review, and he concluded simply be reinstating the Great Tradition of male literature and its male criticism: 'There is no dissociating the aims of the sentimental novel from the aims of a writer like Defoe (as Leo Braudy has shown).' The end of the review differed somewhat from Brophy's and Brookner's 'it should not be done' by asserting 'it cannot be done'. The final putdown was presumably irresistible. Surely a poor female pudding maker could not have taken on herself such a chore as writing an 'introduction to the intellectual history of the time' – and so perhaps it was the publishers, the naughty men, who set her this impossible task.

I put forward this melancholy story not to make any immense claims for these works, not primarily to suggest that I have been around a long time while simultaneously laying hold of the trope of modesty, but simply to indicate, with these very different responses, that the hostility to the whole enterprise of feminist criticism is far greater in Britain than in the USA, both in universities and in the cultural establishment.

Other experiences on both sides of the Atlantic – through the period of feminist agitation into a time when the media is trying to shunt us into a premature post-feminism – have forced me to realize that feminism has made hardly any general headway in Britain, while, in the USA, its gains have been only paper thin. Many have been manipulated and subverted into new oppressions: American divorce practice, for example, seemed to be suggesting a certain equality of men and women with its move to equitable distribution, but it has resulted simply in disadvantaging women left as ever with the children, but often now with nowhere to keep them; the usage change that brought in the unrevealing 'Ms' has made this address the designation mainly of the divorced in Britain.[7]

As for feminist criticism of whatever sort, it has made hardly any headway in institutions in Britain. It has had more success in the polytechnics than in the universities but has not had much anywhere. Where it has been allowed into universities, it has often crept in through a relationship with something called 'literary theory', an abstraction that sinks the heart of Britain's older academic establishments and excites in the newer a hunger for quick significance. So related, feminist criticism may sometimes have slid into the academy, mystified out of politics and revealing no designs on the curriculum or the canon. The American type of socio-historical feminist analysis has hardly flourished anywhere.

In my concentration on the legacy of and development from the earliest socio-historical feminists, I have tried to avoid nostalgia, the location of some utopia in the past, mine or anyone else's, as well as the idealization it causes. But I agree with Cora Kaplan, an American critic working in Britain, who remarks in *Sea Changes* (1986), a collection of her essays over the years, that brutal rejection of the past, of the liberationist political mode and what might now seem the false euphoria of the 1960s and early 1970s, 'sets up another mythology in which these decades appear as a naïve political childhood assessed from a realistic adult perspective' (p. 8). I want to hold onto the past and to historicize it, while avoiding any premature consigning of it to history.

Positions

Since any summary, even an appropriating one, must survey, I will be stating my own position mainly in varying eulogistic or denigratory responses to other people's positions. So it might be as well briefly to anticipate my points.

The feminist critics or commentators on feminist criticism whom I will be mentioning, male and female, are all involved in and engaged by a method, a theory or a vision that is ridiculous or imperceptible to the majority of academics in British and, I suspect, American departments of literature and history. I would rather stand up with any of them – Toril Moi, Terry Eagleton, Alice Jardine or Adrienne Rich, to name only a few – than with the traditional guardians of an excluding culture which it occurs to none of them to interrogate. But, having affirmed solidarity and noted that from a high vantage point we might all seem compatriots, I would like to take issue with those theoretical critics mainly influenced by psychoanalysis and deconstruction who, I believe, have put theory before literature and the idea of woman before the experience of women. I would also like to criticize those socio-historical feminists who have rushed to generalize on the basis of too little history and have consequently fallen into the kind of pervasive dualism that the psychoanalytical critics rightly mock.

Critics like Toril Moi, Mary Jacobus and Alice Jardine make a case for rereading and recuperating Freud, Lacan and Derrida, using all three to help in one of the accepted enterprises of feminist criticism, the demolition of the traditional binary oppositions at the base of our civilization, such as culture and nature, subject and object, reason and emotion, each deriving from the sexist category of dominance. But they make this recuperaton by accepting other scenarios of dominance, less static perhaps but equally firm. For all the feminist transforming, translating and rarifying, at the root of psychoanalysis are those masculine fantasies that make penis envy, sibling rivalry, or the discovery of castration in the mother not only universal stories but also the ground and base of desiring knowledge, a masculine-based sexuality as epistemology. Even if penis envy dwindles into peeing envy or swells into desire for the phallus, the importance of the male organ on which difference is quite arbitrarily based appears to remain absolute.

Psychoanalysis has achieved an extraordinary dominance in certain intellectual circles, seemingly as complete as the hold of Christianity in the Middle Ages; on both systems immense exegetical rather than critical efforts have been expended, which have resulted in much subtle and aesthetically pleasing writing. But the myths that describe its philosophy and programme are hardly unsettled. Psychoanalysis when turned onto history eschews the empirical and so avoids questioning; with its repetition of the oedipal and mirroring dramas of the self and its hierarchical realms of consciousness, it becomes a stranglehold on any apprehension of a self in time, giving a tragic inevitability that aborts political effort and justifies the kind of sophisticated scepticism that is becoming so fashionable in the West. Instead of facilitating political aims it allows us to fall back into a privatizing retreat, to the family and to interiority. Where in all this is the agency, the resistance, the public place of feminism?

When it becomes a theory of criticism, it seems to grow supremely arrogant, knowing its own primacy to the literature it envelops and immediately puncturing surfaces to find a reassuring depth of madness and impotent rage, associating women (or the feminine voice within the text) with the madness and irrationality that men have always been quick to bestow on them. At the same time, it shores up the project of traditional criticism and takes part in the constant evasive and ultimately conservative working over of canonical texts.

I am ending my study with Mary Wollstonecraft because I feel that she expresses something of the enlightenment social hopes, although much disturbed by the gender which most enlightenment thinkers failed to consider. We have moved on from her time and critics influenced by psychoanalysis have found in the once vaunted rationality of the eighteenth century a sublimated sexuality masquerading as the desire to know as well as a naïve acceptance of the myth of the unified subject; for such critics the pursuit of social change has been transformed into yet another expression of the desire for dominance. And yet the enlightenment's political hopes have not been entirely superseded or dislodged by this critique; indeed they cannot be, for the notion of rationality and self-awareness working towards political change forms the only agenda in which there is any chance of progress. Some idea of progress we must have if we do not intend to read, write and struggle in an echoing space.

I should like to see more feminist literary history, aware of the problems of history as different fictions or different discourses, trying within this awareness to provide more detailed specific information on literature in history, and giving women clearer and more various voices than the single ones too quickly discovered in the socio-historical criticism of the American 1970s. I think that literature, specific, detailed, newly found literature, can and should reassert itself and, with its various unassimilable stories and its material uniqueness, cut through the reified premises and notions of psychoanalysis. In the same way the female experience that this literature seeks to convey or make problematic can, I hope, unsettle the deconstruction that aims at its evaporation. With such an agenda feminist criticism stays within feminism, where it belongs.

1

Early Work

To begin inevitably with history, American feminist critical history, it is immediately clear that there really are no great names, no authorities to revere like the French rewriter of Freud, Jacques Lacan, or the philosopher of deconstruction, Jacques Derrida, or indeed like the French women psychoanalytical critics, Luce Irigaray or Julia Kristeva. Partly this reflects the ideals of early American feminist criticism which precisely opposed any authority. In the mid- and late-1970s names such as Elaine Showalter and Sandra Gilbert and Susan Gubar arose which are still current but none can really be said to dominate the field theoretically or methodologically, although each has achieved a position of influence and academic respectability unknown to and unattainable by any primarily feminist scholar in Britain. Their achievement suggests the unparalleled gains of feminist criticism in the States, its extraordinary institutional acceptance from a British standpoint, and its perhaps inevitable collusion with the critical establishment it sought to reform and influence rather than destroy.

In opposition to the French – and to some extent British feminist criticism, a far less influential variety – the American version is historical and empirical in its orientation. In its early phases it stressed intellectual equality and the need for equal opportunity, while downgrading that 'difference' of men and women celebrated by French thinkers. Women were seen as a class more than a caste, distinct only in being universally oppressed.

Given its orientation, the most appropriate way to approach it is historically and contextually, to apply to it the method on which it has usually taken its stand; so I will give it a brief socio-history, allowing it to move towards narrative with all the limiting and even falsifying that that necessarily implies. Mary Jacobus, a British critic who was formerly a member of the Marxist-Feminist Literary Collective although she is now a francophile critic working in the USA, has been in a strong circumstantial position to judge American feminist criticism; she has noted its tendency towards narrative with some disapproval since she sees it as an essentialist – that is biologically determinist – fallacy, a leaning towards the critic's own female experience or 'herstory'. There is considerable truth in the observation; yet, with some acceptance of implications, there may be a way to accept and even celebrate certain non-formalist assumptions about the relation of literature and language to self, experience and history.

Foremothers

Feminist criticism begins, I suppose, when the first woman became aware of her relationship to language and conscious of herself as writer, speaker, reader or auditor. But it probably gets under way in our time with Virginia Woolf's *A Room of One's Own* (1928) and with Simone de Beauvoir's *The Second Sex* (1949). With much simplification and compression, these two books may be seen as begetting the American and French lines of feminist criticism.

Although more systematic than Woolf's, Beauvoir's book is less useful for feminist literary history in its tendency to universalize as nature rather than historicize as culture the distinctions of men and women. Toril Moi, who admires Beauvoir as the precursor and mother of modern feminism, gives her significance as an exemplary woman of rationality, an intellectual woman. Yet she also sees her caught up in a rationality defined by and for men, especially by the existential philosophy of her companion Jean-Paul Sartre. Both trapped in and liberated by the equation of consciousness and maleness, 'Beauvoir cannot appropriate for feminism the Sartrean notion of free *subjectivity* and self-defining agency without becoming "contaminated" by the profoundly sexist ideology of objectivity to which this notion is inevitably coupled.'[1]

There are added problems. In *The Second Sex*, Beauvoir's practice of ransacking culture for myths and constructions of woman diminishes the book's usefulness for women since it focuses on men's needs and habits, while for literary critics it is limited by its philosophical rather than literary approach. In this penchant for the philosophical, it does however foreshadow later French feminist activity which veers into disciplines such as philosophy and psychoanalysis and, even when focusing on feminine writing, usually avoids specific analysis of literary works.

Virginia Woolf is literary through and through, tending towards narrative or story at every turn. She makes ideas into a particular biography and criticism into a kind of life history, most notably in her narrative of the poet, Judith Shakespeare, female equivalent of the famous William; inevitably this woman poet fails before she writes down her poetry, caught firmly in the 'fetish' of chastity. Woolf was wrong when, focusing on the silence of women, she saw no women loving and befriending each other in literature before Jane Austen. But her ignorance of the tradition of women's (and men's) fiction and poetry that extolled female friendship simply exposes the silencing rather than the silence, for few of the early women writers would have been much read by the time she was writing and few were in print. At the same time her lack of knowledge here places her within a tradition of women writers who wanted a history and literature and worried over their absence. It is a long line, stretching at least from the Duchess of Newcastle in the seventeenth century who, excited by her own rational powers, lamented the paucity of creative and rational achievement in her sex.

Woolf has been blamed for being essentialist, believing, for example, in a sentence that in structure and style is recognizably feminine, and for being too individualistic.[2] Certainly her stance was never collective and she promoted private martyrdom amd self-effacement without having any clear notion of how the individual experience could lead to communal acts or indeed to the desired advent of Shakespeare's sister. Certainly too she was writing from a particular class.

All these aspects are limitations but they come with some compensation. Her awareness of her own class-bound situation seems to contribute to her awareness of differences in time and place within a single sex, an awareness that many later feminists dealing only in universals tend to forget.[3] While she was individualistic, she understood that women's common silence had been bound up with sexual conventions and with economic dependence and that speech, where it occasionally existed in the past, had been an act of individual effort against all grains. Criticism became story, perhaps the essentialist story of woman, but, unlike the universal conclusions of Beauvoir, Woolf's narrative of Judith Shakespeare, raped and silenced in the past, pointed to a future in which women should help her to speak.[4]

This is not entirely to give narrative and history to English speakers and essence and philosophy to French. For example, at about the same time as Virginia Woolf was writing, Dorothy Richardson, famous through Woolf for her invention of the elastic and enveloping 'woman's sentence', could make a very different statement about a woman's relationship to privileged art; she declared that no woman, however gifted 'could have brought herself to write "The Intimations of Immortality"', not because she was silenced or overwhelmed by the masculinity of high art but because the shades of the prison house do not close in on her: 'within her is a small gleam of the infinity men seek to catch within the shapes of systems of religion . . .'.[5] None the less, in this continuum from woman as essence, metaphysical signifier of some sort or psychological given, to women of different colours, classes, ages, and places, living in history, it does seem that twentieth-century Anglo-American feminist criticism has leaned towards the edge of history.

Sexual and literary politics

The earliest phase of feminist criticism, inaugurated by activist feminists, is linked with the earliest phase of the modern American feminist movement in the late 1960s, helped along by such works as Betty Friedan's *The Feminine Mystique* (1963). This was a popular reformist rather than revolutionary book with an immensely wide catchment; it is made somewhat depressing now by its author's later trajectory out of feminism, but, in its time, it usefully suggested to women that the problem was not simply patriarchy, the rule of powerful men, but also women's response to it. Consequently there was something they themselves could do. Women had learnt from their participation in the civil rights and anti-war movements that their role had frequently been limited to serving men (Stokeley Carmichael's response in 1964 to a paper on the position of women in the anti-racist Student Non-Violent Coordinating Committee – 'the only position for women in SNCC is prone' – was notorious). Consciousness-raising groups promoted the nascent feminist awareness, along with 1960s style sexual liberation and calls for female sexual, political and psychological power.[6]

Feminist criticism was inaugurated to take part in the activity. It insisted on yoking art and life and was flamboyantly engaged, completely avoiding neutrality and indeed disputing the concept of neutrality for any criticism. Its cry was that the personal was political. Literature in feminist production and consumption became a kind of therapy which undermined the authoritative impersonality of male criticism, apprehended as a weapon of patriarchal control. To avoid colluding with this oppressive criticism, the feminist version became loudly confessional, emphasizing the context and genesis of the criticism and the character and circumstances of the critic. It was loud because there was a feeling, following Woolf, that women had been silent for too long and must now allow a 'sense of wrong, [to be] voiced' as Tillie Olsen expressed it in *Silences* (1972). Canonical literature was ransacked for role models and vilified for the aggression against women it so often held. Meanwhile, formerly quiet works were made to yield a message of disturbance and protest. This excited criticism is partly exemplified by Mary Ellmann's *Thinking about Women* (1968), which mocked assertive masculine criticism and its notions of manliness in style and art. Ellmann, like Woolf, found female expression in a kind of style rather than in the choice of peculiar experience (the later location of the specifically female), and she saw this style providing a subversively different perspective which served to unsettle the fixity of masculine judgement. In many ways Ellmann provided a commonsensical empirical statement of much of what French feminism would elaborately proclaim in the next decade.

Although the wittiest and most subtle of the early political works, Ellmann's book had little immediate impact. The great blockbuster was Kate Millett's *Sexual Politics* (1970). This was the most famous mother of American feminist criticism, translating, in the resonant clichés of *Time Magazine*, 'the war of the sexes from 19th century bedroom farce into raw guerrilla warfare'. Millett made a frontal attack on the overt misogyny of much privileged literature, its use of power and domination in its description of sexual activity, and she saw this writing directly as a source of the physical and psychological oppression of women.

In simple but powerful fashion Millett reinterpreted certain underappreciated works; Charlotte Brontë's *Villette* was rescued from Matthew Arnold's dismissal of it as the vessel of the author's 'hunger, rebellion and rage', or rather it was allowed to yield these qualities in the context of a feminist desire for female autonomy; 'hunger, rebellion and rage' became 'one long meditation on a prison break'. Millett saw the critical fate of Charlotte Brontë as a typical example of masculine critical prejudice and she used *Villette* to show the disjunction between the dominant literary discourse and women's literary response.

Millett's overarching thesis was socio-historical, positing a transformation in the relationship between the sexes during the nineteenth and early twentieth centuries which was followed by a reaction amply expressed in the writings of D. H. Lawrence, Henry Miller and, most recently, Norman Mailer. This reaction prevented any real modification of patriarchy and frustrated revolutionary change. Unproblematically, Millett took literature as mimesis, describing and interpreting life out there, but she did not simply accept the gender oppositions which most of the literature she described conveyed. In her view gender became a psychological concept referring to culturally acquired sexual identity, not a natural given, as women had been hoodwinked into thinking. In her concluding section she showed, through the homosexual novels and plays of Jean Genet, how frighteningly easy gender identity was to lose and how much the terms masculine and feminine had simply come to encode notions of high and low, master and slave.

Although colloquial in tone, Millett's *Sexual Politics* is recognizably academic; it is footnoted and addressed to an educated middle class reader sharing a common culture. Yet it was quickly denounced as unscholarly by Norman Mailer, one of its victims; in *The Prisoner of Sex* (1971) he accused it of being unscholarly in its imprecise generalizations and its habit of reading passages out of context. Other feminists pointed out its misinterpretation of *Villette*, its tendency to ignore the literary aspect of literature, as well as its habit of making patriarchy universal. Certainly there was a naïve collapsing of character and author, as in most early feminist readings, similar to the collapsing of reader and author in the excitement of response. But, whatever its failings, the book was absolutely pertinent and of its time, and it did good service in revealing the old fashioned libertine aspects of the libertarian 1960s, with its gurus, Wilhelm Reich and Herbert Marcuse, and its literary heroes, Miller and Mailer.

The early phase of feminist criticism occurred towards the end of a time of civil disruption on American university campuses. In contrast to Britain, institutions were so large, numerous and affluent that the student body formed a political force. The curriculum of literary study, less culturally secure than in Britain, was modifiable and could for a time respond to student enthusiasm. The criticism of the early and mid-1970s was, then, often tied to consciousness-raising activities in the classroom and to straightforward reformist desires to teach and hear something good about women and something bad about men. And it was also tied to certain folklore activities of feminism much enjoyed by the press. The pedagogical aim and popular alliance are responsible for a great deal of the mockery with which feminist literary study has been received by those who believe in a traditional canon of English literary excellence and in transcendental principles of taste.

Millett's *Sexual Politics* helped to give an evangelical feeling to the early movement of feminist criticism. Acceptance became a kind of awakening, a change of vision or re-vision to use Adrienne Rich's term, and much women's criticism, like Methodist autobiographies, took the form of life histories detailing a progress into critical light. Understanding was awareness of the politics within the literary, the misogyny at the heart of so much that was culturally privileged, misogyny that had become psychological and social oppression from which women needed liberation. Criticism following Millett concentrated on reducing canonical works to their predictable structures, their common visions, both of male quests for what was frequently envisaged as not woman and of contingent women as angels and whores, and it tied these representations to life, so revealing how the literary harshness was further expressed in social discrimination. The degradation of women in fiction, especially in pornography, was similar to the degradation of women in the streets; rape was rampant in literature and life, and the influence was in both directions. Literature was peculiarly implicated in the general oppression, then, because it had colonized the minds of both sexes with those stereotypes that had kept each gender firmly in place. Only through literary analysis, largely the domain of men until this time, could this power be controlled, and in such analysis it was necessary to see gender as the most basic definition and distinction and to understand that its transparency had been an immense deception.

Since the canon of literature in English represented power, the concentration in these early days was on the classic texts. They were given alternative readings either to resurrect them or to reveal their pernicious centres. The activity was most intense on American literature which was peculiarly male-centered and misogynist – English literature, more entrenched, has on the whole been reinterpreted, not opposed. During the next decade, the attack moved to encompass male criticism as well as male creative works. Annette Kolodny (*The Lay of the Land*, 1975) and Judith Fetterley (*The Resisting Reader*, 1978) showed the extent of the cultural betrayal of women in both literature and its study. The assumption had been absolute that the reader was male, an assumption simply reinforced by later critics using Stanley Fish's reader response theory. Harold Bloom had declared portentously, 'That which you are, that only can you read'. Quite so, was the feminist response. Fetterley's book was intended not simply as traditional literary criticism but also as a liberating act for women and a survival manual for the female reader facing a literature that had become a zone of combat.

The prescriptive criticism of major literary authorities was seen not only to depend on and to canonize certain male writers like Melville and Hawthorne, notoriously hostile to women authors, but to work against any appreciation of those genres in which women chose or were forced to write. Nina Baym noted how, although commercially and numerically women had probably dominated American literature, at least from the mid nineteenth-century, theories controlling the reading of this literature excluded from critical comment those popular women authors, like Fanny Fern of the 1850s, who wrote specifically for women. Jane Tompkins pointed out that the privileging of certain modes of male writing banished the phenomenally successful female sentimental writers like Harriet Beecher Stowe from the canon. Male critics such as Lionel Trilling, Leslie Fiedler and Sacvan Bercovich were judged to have found the essence of Americanism in precisely those themes and methods associated with men. In both literature and its criticism, women had become associated not with culture but with the impediments to it and the essence of American writing had been discovered in the male struggle for integrity and artistry precisely against woman and the woman writer. On the other side, female writing that did not conform to the stereotype of what was considered pap literature had had difficulty finding a critical audience at all; Charlotte Perkins Gilman's powerful short story, *The Yellow Wallpaper*, was misread because of the lack of those connections with the horror tradition of Poe that would have been made for male writing. The majority of women writers had been seen as 'isolate islands of symbolic significance, available only to, and decipherable only by, one another'.[7] A revisionist rereading of the entire literary inheritance of American literature, male and female, was required.

A woman's tradition

By this stage the canon itself was under attack both by those who wanted to insert women and by those who desired to form an alternative canon. As in the earliest feminist studies of male literature, so in women's, the first books were in the mode of the rhapsodic, inspired by the heady atmosphere of the newly liberated feminist classroom.

Patricia Spacks in *The Female Imagination* (1975), described the literature of female experience and its excited consumption by newly conscious women students. The book asked huge questions such as 'Do any characteristic patterns of self-perception shape the creative experience of women?' although it sidled away from either asserting or denying the genderized imagination its title declared. Like *Sexual Politics* it assumed that novels referred directly to the world or to the self of the writer but it fell short of specific historicizing of that world or the self. Like the books of Millett and Ellmann, it concentrated on the nineteenth and twentieth centuries although a later work, *Imagining a Self* (1976) discussing Fanny Burney and the eighteenth century, to some extent compensated for this bias.

By now the emphasis was firmly on the distinction of female from male subject-matter. Ellen Moers's *Literary Women* (1976) linked female characters and authors as heroines in the march of female history, positing a female tradition of influence by the side of men's and discovering female modes and myths in literature. With an unusually wide reference extending to European as well as English and American literature, Moers was concerned to place the most known women writers within rich groupings of other neglected women: 'It can be argued that Jane Austen achieved the classical perfection of her fiction because there was a mass of women's novels, excellent, fair, and wretched, for her to study and improve upon. Mary Brunton and the rest of the ladies were her own kind; she was at ease with them' (p. 44).

Like *The Female Imagination*, Moers's book is both conventionally academic in its use of footnotes and abstractions and distinctively fashionable in its presenting of the critic herself. Indeed it is this picture of the writer situated in a specific time that makes much of the work's fascination, especially her obvious and direct engagement with literature and her sense of herself in the 'living literary history of the period of my work on this book'. The presentation is self-conscious but still appealing; she lets us know that she is on the lecture circuit, that she shattered the calm of the splendid chamber in the New York Public Library by laughing aloud at Fanny Burney's unpublished play *The Witlings*, and that she made her pilgrimage to George Sand's *Vallée-Noire*. It is sad that the vibrant Ellen Moers died so young.

To this phase of feminist criticism Elaine Showalter contributed *A Literature of Their Own* (1977) in which she discovered a female subculture in the domestic fiction of minor nineteenth-century English women writers. Her book made no aesthetic case for the critically ignored genre these women chose, but focused instead on the social context and guilt of the enterprise. Showalter was wary of the implications in Moers and Spacks that there was a separate and continuous tradition of women writers:

> The book is an effort to describe the female literary tradition in the English novel from the generation of the Brontës to the present day, and to show how the development of this tradition is similar to the development of any literary subculture. Women have generally been regarded as 'sociological chameleons,' taking on the class, lifestyle, and culture of their male relatives. It can, however, be argued that women themselves have constituted a subculture within the framework of a larger society, and have been unifed by values, conventions, experiences, and behaviors impinging on each individual. It is important to see the female literary tradition in these broad terms, in relation to the wider evolution of women's self-awareness and to the ways in which any minority group finds its direction of self-expression relative to a dominant society, because we cannot show a pattern of deliberate progress and accumulation. It is true, as Ellen Moers writes, that 'women studied with a special closeness the works written by their own sex'; in terms of influences, borrowings, and affinities, the tradition is strongly marked. But it is also full of holes and hiatuses, because of what Germaine Greer calls the 'phenomenon of the transience of female literary fame'; 'almost uninterruptedly since the Interregnum, a small group of women have enjoyed dazzling literary prestige during their own lifetimes, only to vanish without trace from the records of posterity'. Thus each generation of women writers has found itself, in a sense, without a history, forced to rediscover the past anew, forging again and again the consciousness of their sex. Given this perpetual disruption, and also the self-hatred that has alienated women writers from a sense of collective identity, it does not seem possible to speak of a 'movement' (p. 12).

Showalter's historical thesis derived from the emergence of black consciousness. The phases she found were three. First, the feminine, in which the woman tried to equal male achievement by internalizing the assumptions of male culture; second, the didactic feminist, when women rejected the accommodation of femininity and used literature to dramatize the ordeals of wronged womanhood, and finally the female, turning to woman's experience as a source of autonomous art. This tripartite (Hegelian) structure would be recurrent in Showalter's work.

Despite its apparent emphasis on history, the book stayed firmly in the nineteenth century, ignoring the wealth of earlier writing by women which Moers touched on and which would greatly have modified its thesis. So Showalter can declare that women did not think of themselves as professional writers before 1800, when there are in fact hosts of professional novelists in the eighteenth century as well as dramatists from the Restoration onwards. In this concentration on the Victorian period and on the mode of domestic realism, as well as in its ignoring of the problem of aesthetic judgement and language, *A Literature of Their Own* was typical of the early phase of feminist criticism on women. It represented the most useful beginning of socio-historical scholarship but its omissions skewed the understanding of the female past and encouraged premature generalization that did duty for specific history.

The critical reappraisal of female writing, typified by Showalter, was liberal and humanist in its assumptions. It was as political as the reappraisal of male literature. It indicated that the culture represented its past as male, that half of humanity was hardly included, and that a reimagining of the literary tradition was long overdue. It took some ammunition from *A Room of One's Own* with its desire for a rewriting of history and it might be summarized in Carolyn Heilbrun's words in 'Bringing the spirit back to English Studies' (1979) as a revitalization of literature , an attempt to give it a new moral and cultural authority, not through the expression of a tradition, as in Matthew Arnold and F. R. Leavis, but through revolutionary activity. Western culture was no longer seen as a republic of letters to which both sexes were equal heirs but as a state in which the rulers were usurping men who had recreated women in alienated terms as nature, inspiration or chaos. At a time when literature was losing its humanist rationale, Heilbrun tried to co-opt the humanist position for feminism, announcing ringingly: 'feminism, able to combine structuralism, historical criticism, New

Criticism, and deconstructionism, reaches into our past to offer, through fundamental reinterpretation, a new approach to literary studies. Moreover, it offers vitality to counter what threatens us: the exhaustibility of our subject' (p. 23).

The culmination of this period was probably Sandra Gilbert and Susan Gubar's *The Madwoman in the Attic* (1979), a hybrid work which moves from the historical emphasis of Showalter and focuses less on her little known writers than on the approved authors like Jane Austen, the Brontës and George Eliot. Based on Harold Bloom's Freudian reading of literature as the record of the oedipal anxiety of writers in the shadow of their predecessors, it tried to look behind the surface markers of literature and culture for some essential pattern of repetition, the suppressed female, the sense of the hidden and denied. Through close readings of texts already accepted as canonical by traditional criticism, the authors showed how women writers responded to socio-cultural constraints by creating symbolic narratives that expressed their common feelings of constriction, exclusion and dispossession. Over and over again the mad Bertha of Charlotte Brontë's *Jane Eyre* was found to be the double of the sane and decorous spinster heroine who could only contemplate such madness in her fantastic dreams. So resonant was the idea, so well chosen the title, that it generated variations, the most recent of which is Germaine Greer's title for her essays depicting her progress through the feminist years, *The Madwoman's Underclothes*.

Although they eschewed the socio-historical method of Showalter, Gilbert and Gubar are firmly in the 1970s mode. They aimed to expose 'a common, female impulse to struggle free from social and literary confinement through strategic redefinitions of self, art, and society' (p. xii). Texts were seen as 'palimpsestic' with surface designs that concealed or obscured deeper, less accessible levels of meaning. The aim was described in a 1980 essay of Sandra Gilbert, 'to decode and demystify all the disguised questions and answers that have always shadowed the connections between textuality and sexuality, genre and gender, psychosexual identity and cultural authority'.

It was an exciting book, the impact of which was similar in strength to that of Millett's a decade before. Some of this excitement was generated simply by the fact that the bookl was a *tour de force*, enormous, monothematic, bristling with allusions, and enjoyably clever. Yet, when one had recovered from the excitement, it was clear that something had been lost in the achievement.

For a start the actual number of women discussed was very small and, unlike Showalter's group, they tended to be precisely those authors already privileged by male literary scholarship. By concentrating on common patterns, the authors provided little sense of the rich, varied and often extremely opaque texture of women's writing through the centuries. When the fact of this small corpus is added to the selection of the nineteenth century as the starting place, it becomes clear that some violence has had to be done against history and the hundreds of women writers before Jane Austen – and indeed after – who might not have fitted into the established psychological pattern and who might not be represented by their dominant sisters. In addition, the psyches of the chosen women exist in a kind of vacuum, the material world having been largely elided. Or rather they exist solely in the realm of impulse and ideas, ideas dominated by twentieth-century psychology and literary criticism. The resistance that is found in the works is always covert and mental; as Marilyn Butler has noted in her preface to the reissue of her *Jane Austen and the War of Ideas* (1975), 'It is . . . a major distraction that twentieth-century critical discourse has so firmly valorised rebellion in the head rather than rebellion on the streets'.

Inevitably, with their model taken from the present, Gilbert and Gubar are more convincing on later periods than on Jane Austen. With this early writer further historical and literary historical placing would have revealed how often what the authors take as idiosyncratic vision is common currency and derives from the genre of women's fiction in which she was writing. Frequently indeed the Jane Austen whom they discover on the edge of containing her aggression might with more literary context be found modifying the radical content of the novel she had inherited. To put her in the world of Mary Wollstonecraft, Charlotte Smith, Elizabeth Inchbald, Maria Edgeworth and Fanny Burney is to see what chances for protest and aggressive complaint she intentionally missed, while her placing in the world of the peasant John Clare and the milkwoman Ann Yearsley might have indicated how much she expressed her class as well as her gender.

I wish then that Gilbert and Gubar had provided more history and let in more variation and that the madwoman had been allowed to live a little outside the attic in her particular society. None the less, my wish does not prevent my admiring this cumbersome – Gilbert and Gubar have a propensity for the monstrously large in books – enlivening and inspiring work. If its influence tended to make the necessary historical endeavour seem commonplace and uninteresting, it yet established other possibilities in criticism, and its own theatrical historical intervention, its livening up of the subject, cannot be underestimated.

Mothers and myths

Towards the end of this heroic phase of feminist criticism came a stress on the difference between men and women, although individual differences among women remained underplayed. Perhaps the earliest feminist period, overlapping with the civil rights movement in the States and to some extent growing from it, had inevitably feared any emphasis on the difference that, in black and white terms, had been translated into the notoriously discriminatory formula, 'separate but equal'. In the mid-1970s, however, along with the continuing emphasis on equal rights and opportunites, there was a new celebration of the distinctive experience of woman. For this celebration, history with its monotonous record of oppression and repression was not enough and a mythological excitement developed.

Obviously there was some dependence on male myth criticism, in vogue in the 1950s and 1960s, especially after Northrop Frye's *Anatomy of Criticism* (1957), but the motifs and messages were feminist. Above all motherhood came to the fore, remembered, anticipated, investigated, eulogized and mythologized. Maternal and fertility rituals became a feature of women's college campuses and literature was pressed into the service of the hidden mother goddess.

In this heady atmosphere the poet and critic Adrienne Rich produced *Of Woman Born* (1976) praising motherhood, creativity, female bonding, and the lesbian experience all in one and dreamt of a common language uncovering the female self. Clearly the feminist mood had changed since 1970 when, inspired simply by anger at women's continual and continuing subordination, Shulamith Firestone in *The Dialectic of Sex* could find oppressive anything that separated women from men and could look forward to a period when scientific advances would relieve women of reproduction altogether. Rich, in contrast, praised a freely chosen motherhood and saw it as the metaphor of female relationships.

In *Feminist Criticism: Women as Contemporary Critic* (1986), Maggie Humm, a great admirer of Adrienne Rich, describes a woman-centered project very similar to Rich's (perhaps it is her rather unquestioning admiration that gives her book a curiously dated quality – as well as a friendliness somewhat rare in recent books of feminist theory): 'My own feeling is that feminist literary critics must enjoy being women and being with other women. They must enjoy reading the work of women writers and helping other women to enjoy reading women's literature. They must be women choosing to read women as women.' In *On Lies, Secrets, and Silence* (1979), her selected prose written between 1966 and 1978, Rich defined a female consciousness which was 'political, aesthetic, and erotic, and which refuses to be included or contained in the culture of passivity'. Re-vision, the new way of reading and looking, was to discover a new psychic space, a new history and a new language, bringing together ethics, living and thinking. Rich's achievement, according to Humm, was 'a challenging libidinal theory of radical feminism' ('radical' having by the 1980s come to denote female difference, often a belief in separatist solutions) and 'an almost pantheistic celebration of female history' (pp. 178 and 197).

Nancy Chodorow's *The Reproduction of Mothering* (1978) and 'Gender, Relation, and Difference in Psychoanalytic Perspective' (1980) further celebrated motherhood by revising the traditional Freudian psychology which concentrated on the male oedipal drama and assigned penis envy to the girl. Chodorow, in contrast to Freud, connected the child's sense of identity with the mother. The subject's growth, that is, the differentiation or perception of demarcation of the self and the object world, occurred in relation to the mother; consequently it became the boy who had to learn individual identity negatively and whose difference required constant reinforcement. The troubles of the girl, whose identity was built on sameness since it did not, like the boy's, contradict the primary sense of oneness and identification with the mother, began after the oedipal phase when difference was given a new value through male socio-cultural hegemony and when women's self-definition was oriented to men. Chodorow escaped the Freudian notion of the unconscious and favoured instead an idea of gender imprinting and role-playing. The idea found considerable acceptance in the States since it connected the unmodifiable psychological with the more accessible sociological. With its emphasis on cultural context – which could of course be changed in some way – it allowed an optimism in keeping with the early days of feminism but incompatible with the unrevised Freudian tragedy.

The most influential of these early revisers of male myths, psychoanalytical or literary, was undoubtedly Mary Daly, an immensely popular figure among women students on American campuses in the 1970s. In *Beyond God the Father* (1973) Daly accused men of having stolen language from women, a theft enacted in *Genesis*. Consequently women must transform and take back their language. In *Gyn/Ecology* she aimed to move beyond the male myths encoded within the language and beyond a male-centered logic of binary opposites based on the gender division to form a new female syntax which would naturally express the female body.

Although Dorothy Dinnerstein in *The Mermaid and the Minotaur* (1976), which belongs to this sort of writing, emphasized gender as socially constructed, it was on the whole true of this group that it did not interrogate history or consider how myths and explanatory fables had come to be created in the first place. The result was not so much analysis as the creation of counter myths, with past literature being either dropped or prodded to provide utopian visions.

The presentation was similarly reactive. It made a point of stressing its distinction from male scholarship. 'It seemed to me impossible from the first to write a book of this kind without being often autobiographical, without often saying "I". Yet for many months I buried my head in historical research and analysis in order to delay . . . the plunge into areas of my own life which were painful and problematical, yet from the heart of which this book has come,' wrote Adrienne Rich about *Of Woman Born* (pp. 15–16). The claim was to amateur status not scholarship. Dinnerstein too insisted that she was unsystematic: 'Any effort to form a rational policy about what to take in, out of the inhuman flood of printed human utterance that pours over us daily, feels to me like a self-deluded exercise in pseudomastery' (pp. viii–ix).

It was all very exciting at the time. The personal, the assertive, and the provocative were, for most of us, new modes for women and they seemed wonderfully liberating. Something of the exciting assertiveness of early American feminist criticism is caught in the absolute openings of the most famous texts, a rebellion against the impersonal, overly careful, conventional style that we had all been taught in the 1950s and early 1960s to deliver and receive. So Kate Millett begins *Sexual Politics* with a quotation from Henry Miller: 'I would ask her to prepare the bath for me. She would pretend to demur but she would do it just the same.' Inevitably 'she' is pulled into the bath despite her silk stockings and becomes 'a bitch in heat', only the female reader being left to wonder what holds up the stockings in this classic male fantasy. Ellen Moers opens with 'The subject of this book is the major women writers, writers we read and shall always read whether interested or not in the fact that they happen to be women. But the fact of their sex is, frankly, fascinating'. Adrienne Rich begins, 'All human life on the planet is born of woman', while Gilbert and Gubar famously open with 'Is the pen a metaphorical penis?'

2
Consolidation and Reaction

Anxiety

American feminist criticism did not travel well. In Europe it appeared simplistic, associated with the enthusiastic but politically naïve democratization of American higher education in the late 1960s and 1970s and with the self-indulgent desire of some middle-class women to discover role models in literature through simplifying and distorting interpretations. Although it was vaguely historical, it was not historically specific, so that it was of necessity open to charges of exclusivity and cultural bias. Meanwhile there appeared little understanding of the working of ideology or of language, and the concept of the canon of great English literature in particular remained in place, enriched perhaps by a few women whose writing was as close as possible to the aesthetic standards of canonized male work. American feminist criticism often seemed a simple response to literature in countries where socio-political analysis usually relied on a sophisticated Marxist intellectual tradition.

To many in an increasingly anti-American climate towards the end of the 1970s American feminist criticism simply appeared yet another example of cultural imperialism and enviable power. The form that was most available outside the country was connected with privileged WASP or, more frequently, Jewish American women, often enviably affluent and institutionally secure. For American criticism always had a definite institutional base and most of its practitioners were within universities. In the rest of the world there was no equivalence for this privileged base and consequently considerable envy and conde-scension.

To many traditional critics in the USA itself, early feminist analysis seemed a ghastly subversion of all that was rigorous and manly, a fragmenting of the culture that had taken 2,000 years to build and an attack on what J. Hillis Miller proudly called the established canon of English literature. Harold Bloom in *A Map of Misreading* (1975) saw a dreadful possibility of liberated women dominating the West and of men from Homer onwards losing their authority over human studies, rather as Samuel Johnson in 1753 had feared a feminization of culture brought about by the new women writers, the 'Amazons of the pen'.

Uneasiness at the institutional success of this criticism was shared by some American feminist critics. By the late 1970s Women's Studies courses were firmly established in many colleges and universities and Lillian S. Robinson, one of the few early American critics to insist on class as a factor of analysis in feminist criticism, was especially disturbed. In *Sex, Class and Culture* (1978), she worried that the establishment might lead to a co-optation by the very institutions that feminist analysis was designed to subvert, considering that 'the best goals of the movement were diametrically opposed to those of the defining institutions in class society' (p. xxiii). While most later critics of the early American project were inveighing against its political content, throughout the next decade Robinson would continue to insist that it was not political enough; in the introduction to the paperback edition of her book in 1986 she reiterated her original view 'that a women's movement with actual or potential revolutionary power was coming into being, that intellectual and theoretical work – women's studies – could play an important role in that movement, and that, similarly, the study of literature could be a significant mode of apprehending the lives and consciousness of women' (p. xxxi). Robinson's emphasis was cogent and passionately placed, but her route towards activity beyond academic institutions and towards a feminist analysis that included class as well as gender was taken by few American feminists over the next years; her view 'that criticism whose historical insensitivity makes it impossible for the movement to use . . . is not professionally useful either' (p. 65) was persuasive but it was never the dominant one.

Acrimony

Despite the early emphasis on sisterhood, there was considerable acrimony over literary texts, personalities and political stance (although Americans could not compete with the flamboyant nastiness rampant in French feminist circles at the same time). With the flourishing of feminist criticism, a new world of reference had been established. *Villette* was *the* feminist novel, 'Aurora Leigh' the poem and Virginia Woolf the queen or the joker. It was important to get it right on all these topics, but attitudes to Virginia Woolf became the real acid test of critical positions. The situation can be illustrated through Elaine Showalter.

In *A Literature of Their Own*, already a snub, many thought, to the original Woolfian text, *A Room of One's Own*, Virginia Woolf was trounced for evading the problem of femaleness in her projection of the disturbing and dark aspects of a woman's psyche onto men. She was also taken to task for her transformation of the female space into a prison and ultimately a grave. And, Showalter added with a characteristic sally, she helped to make suicide one of 'Bloomsbury's representative art forms'. This spirited and rather muddled attack – Woolf seemed culpable because she supported an androgyny which Showalter rather than Woolf defined and because she was writing both as a man *and* as a woman – was much resented by other critics like Carolyn Heilbrun who greatly admired Woolf's conception of female writing and indeed of androgyny or like Jane Marcus who appreciated what she regarded as Woolf's strenuously achieved political vision.

Another source of acrimony, as well as of awareness, was the lesbian response. As an outspoken lesbian, Adrienne Rich insisted that all women existed on a lesbian continuum, a reasonable view in the context of her definitions of female relationships. In 'Compulsory Heterosexuality and Lesbian Existence' (1980) she went further, however, and discussed the economic, political and ideological factors enforcing heterosexuality on women. In support of her argument she criticized the common habit of identifying the biological processes of impregnation with the emotional and sexual relationships with men. These pronouncements and criticisms were considered hopelessly prescriptive and stultifying by many heterosexual feminists.[1]

Meanwhile, critics who wrote outside the lesbian experience and largely ignored it, like Showalter, Moers, and Gilbert and Gubar, were abused as homophobic, blinded by 'the perceptual screen of heterosexism'. Their enterprise was labelled exclusive: 'All the faults of male critics with respect to women's writing generally are reproduced by some feminist critics with respect to lesbian or black writing,' Mary

Eagleton charged in 1986 when she assessed this early period (p. 3). In the same year, when Showalter compiled her anthology of essays on feminist criticism through the decade, she took care to include token examples of both lesbian and black feminist work.[2] Probably women who represent the majority of feminist critics have yet fully to appreciate the vision of women who are doubly marginal and who have been for a long time aware of the awkward ties of all women to the dominant culture and its language. None the less the wholesale criticism seems excessive. Showalter, Moers, Spacks, Gilbert and Gubar may have been shortsighted or partially blind – clearly they were so in many different ways – but 'homophobic' and 'racist' do not appear helpful or appropriate adjectives for them.

These early critics were further blamed for their style. Still recognizably academic, it was castigated as a collusion with male authority. Jane Rule's *Lesbian Images* (1975), lacking conventional scholarship and analysis, avoided the collusion and did not receive the institutional attention of Showalter's work, for example. During the whole of the 1970s dislike of male scholarship, logic and authority made some American criticism over personal, gushing and woolly. Yet any disapproving response, suggestion or rejection became a hostile patriarchal act.[3]

The fairly crude emphasis on gender difference in early American feminism typical of such writers as Adrienne Rich and Susan Griffin seemed stimulating and provocative at the time but, as a new conservatism succeeded to a seemingly outdated liberation in the 1980s, the emphasis on motherhood, female virtue and natural association, eagerly assigned by eighteenth- and nineteenth-century men to women, fed easily into reaction and traditional restatement. Betty Friedan foresook her reformist political 'first stage' and wrote *The Second Stage* (1981) in which she discovered the enemy no longer in the 'feminine mystique' but instead in the feminist mystique and she proclaimed the family and woman's special qualities. The even more reactionary 'feminist' Jean Bethke Elshtain in *Public Man, Private Woman* (1981), proudly asserted the biological difference, along with the given order and the wonders of motherhood; the saving of society was to occur in the female sphere of the home, marriage and the family, the last haven in the impersonal worlds that had been created by capitalist and socialist alike. The nadir was (possibly) reached in Carol McMillan's *Women, Reason and Nature* (1982) where sexual differences are the human condition, where woman is celebrated in her relation to nature and indissolubly linked with the life process through her reproductive role. Feminism of the 1970s sort has here become a manifestation of the modern alienation from nature, while the male technological medical advance, so welcomed by Shulamith Firestone, is abjured, along with the control of reproduction it allows.[4] It is a long way from Rich, Daly and Griffin, but there is, unhappily, a route between the groups.

Deconstruction

In the late 1970s, in a harsher political and academic climate, the seeming naïvety of American feminist criticism was abandoned, and it turned to enter the theoretical storms which had raged in English departments ever since sputnik had turned science into the only prestigious pursuit for an American academic. Literary criticism had for some years sought to make itself intellectually respectable with the help of other disciplines such as philosophy and sociology. The effort was clearest in the new criticism, termed indiscriminately post-structuralism and deconstruction.

This was associated with Jacques Derrida, working originally from France but increasingly present in the States, and with men connected with Yale University such as Paul de Man, Geoffrey Hartman and J. Hillis Miller. They wrote out of a wider philosophical European tradition than most Anglo-American scholars and were little concerned with the specificities of British or American culture in history. In the 1970s they firmly struck the literary critical consciousness of the States killing off the simple writer in a particular midland village and 'problematizing' – bringing to high self-consciousness – the act of reading.

The French critic, Roland Barthes, proclaimed the death of the author in his celebrated essay of 1968, while Geoffrey Hartman, throwing off a critical 'inferiority complex', installed the critic–reader in the place of the writer: 'We have entered an era that can challenge even the priority of literary to literary-critical texts', he proclaimed in *The Fate of Reading and Other Essays* (1975), p.18. In *Criticism in the Wilderness* (1980), he rejected the traditions of British empiricism and practical criticism, shifting from reason to rhetoric and making the critic equal with the literary work. History and politics naturally fell from the formulation.

The act of interpretation became 'hermeneutics' and attention was switched from Marxist or other political or materialist analysis (although this continued in some form in Derrida's work) to rhetoric, metaphor, catachresis and figurative devices, now regarded as the grounds of all texts. Knowledge was considered to have no absolute purchase on the material world, and the empirical rationalist traditions of the British and French enlightenment gave way to a post-Kantian view that knowledge was only the product of the human mind, an interpretation not a description of the world.

Derrida showed that there was no natural centre in philosophy, no transcendental signifier whether called nature, God or indeed Man, only a habit of privileging certain signifiers, certain words. With no centre and no origin, all became discourse, and binary oppositions that appeared to structure the mental and physical world, like nature and culture, man and woman, lost their absolute meaning; each part took its significance not now through single opposition but through *différance*, open-ended differentiation from all other parts.

For Derrida in particular, all texts, philosophical, scientific, critical and literary, opened themselves to rhetorical questioning and deconstruction, under the notion that writing 'with its own dialectic of blindness and insight, precedes all the categories that conventional wisdom has tried to impose on it.'[5] The critic sought not to understand the presumed intention of the author, now deposed, nor the peculiar inscriptions of a particular time and place, but instead probed texts for insights, moments of conceptual blindness, and gaps in meaning. Deconstruction was described by Barbara Johnson as a 'careful teasing out of warring forces of signification within the text'; a deconstructive reading was 'a reading that analyses the specificity of a text's critical difference from itself', what it knows but cannot itself say.[6]

The feminist response

The methods suggested by deconstruction and the epistemological revolution it assumed seemed immensely liberating to literary studies, and its language and concerns clearly entered American feminist criticism. Indeed the most modest empiricists took on its tinge. In its light the early work of feminist criticism seemed too political, simplistic and static, still regarding literature as works not texts, valorizing the theme and ignoring what was now called textuality. One can turn, as so often, to the reactive Showalter for a response.

In 1979, as the theoretical material was bombarding English departments, she published an essay entitled 'Toward a Feminist Poetics' in which she acknowledged the new methods and, in keeping with her usual socio-cultural ways, contextualized the debates:

> In a shrinking job market, these new levels of professionalization also function as discriminators between the marketable and the marginal lecturer. Literary science, in its manic generation of difficult terminology, its establishment of seminars and institutes of postgraduate study, creates an elite corps of specialists who spend more and more time mastering the theory, less and less reading the books. We are moving towards a two-tiered system of 'higher' and 'lower' criticism, the higher concerned with the 'scientific' problems of form and structure, the 'lower' concerned with the 'humanistic' problems of content and interpretation. And these levels . . . are now taking on subtle gender identities and assuming a sexual polarity – hermeneutics and hismeneutics. Ironically, the existence of a new criticism practiced by women has made it even more possible for structuralism and Marxism to strive, Henchard-like, for systems of formal obligation and determination. Feminists writing in these modes . . . risk being allotted the symbolic ghettos of the special issue or the back of the book for their essays (p. 140).

Placing feminist criticism with deconstruction among the new critical approaches, she argued that feminist criticism was the most isolated and least understood, the most vulnerable to extreme and coarse attacks precisely because of its absence of a clearly articulated method, an absence directly attributable to its early suspicion of all theory. But, understanding the need to define and delimit, she decided to provide not a new theory but a description of practice, a taxonomy, rather as she had earlier done in her feminist literary history, *A Literature of Their Own*. Her project accepted the change in emphasis from literary works to criticism, from literary themes and personal and political implications to the act of writing and the act of reading; the change gave the project a new eclectic, almost reactionary as well as reactive flavour.

In her effort to make the feminist enterprise sound rigorous, Showalter divided feminist criticism into two areas. The first, labelled the feminist critique, concerned the woman as reader, the way the hypothesis of the female reader changes the apprehension of a text and probes the 'ideological assumptions of literary phenomena'. The second concerned the woman as writer and the problems of female creativity and language. This she named gynocritics. Both types of criticism were said to be political and polemical, affiliated to but not dominated by Marxist sociology and aesthetics. In this essay Showalter privileged gynocritics over feminist critique since she found the latter inevitably male oriented, the study of what men have experienced and thought women to be, and she considered the approach in its recent manifestations too dependent on established male critics and their privileged literary discourses.

In opposition gynocritics aims less to deconstruct than to construct. A female framework is required for the analysis of women's writings and new models should be developed, based on the study of female experience rather than on male models and theories. Without the framework of female culture, a critic can misinterpret as well as ventriloquize the notions of male literary history, the periodization of which is completely inappropriate to women's literature.

Despite a stated opposition, already in this essay Showalter's language showed the influence of the new methodologies in a certain instability. The idea of woman as reader and subject, now called woman as sign in a semiotic system, would once simply have been included in images of women in literature, while the fissures in literary history would have been familiar as the exclusion of women. Similarly, what had been woman as writer became woman as the 'producer of textual meaning'. The effect is an appearance of theory with a certain simplification of socio-cultural method and content.

But there are ideological problems beyond uneasiness of style. If the emphasis had remained on history, it is hard to see how feminist critique and gynocritics could actually have been separated in the manner Showalter intended, since the subtle and delicate connection of literature and consciousness, gender and language, cannot easily be investigated where a critic is confined to a particular method and set of works. The woman writer of the eighteenth century, a period which the Victorian-based Showalter largely ignored, is related to male writers like Richardson in a way that can hardly be disentangled without careful reading of his as well as her works, while the gender polarities of that century cut across sex lines to label his prose 'feminine'.

The demand for gynocritics implies a worrying assumption that the investigation of the dominant culture has been concluded. Yet, even in Showalter's formulation, the enterprise of gynocritics must take place within, alongside, beneath or above the still pervasive patriarchal culture, the deconstruction of which has surely much distance to travel. The very fact of feminist criticism's physical location in the academy ought to have made clear its relationship to that academy; the prevailing ideologies have perhaps been slightly shaken but they are still firmly established and it is decidedly premature to foreclose on the effort to shake them further, unless there exist alternative academies with alternative funding.

Finally, Showalter's essay tends in its polemical platform to fall into the utopian longings that she elsewhere criticizes as historically determined and which, when related to literature, inevitably privilege the present at the expense of a benighted past. So in the essay she accepts that much past literature by women has been 'scenarios of compromise, madness, and death' and then she yearns for the transformation of pain into history which she finds in the newest writing. She eulogizes the 'purposeful awakenings', the 'reinvigorated mythologies of female culture' such as those she discovers in Adrienne Rich's *Of Woman Born* which turns old-fashioned matrophobia into the sympathetic quest for the mother.[7]

In her essay Showalter has created a pattern of historical critical phases similar to the one she had earlier used to describe women's literary history in *A Literature of Their Own*; the possible implication here is that, like the earlier paradigm, the critical one suggests a history that is progressing through greater and greater improvements and moving towards more intense consciousness.[8] (This same tripartite pattern recurs in *The Female Malady* (1985) in which attitudes to madness again neatly form themselves into three phases separated by three ideological revolutions.)

In the end the demand for gynocritics separate from feminist critique, buttressed though it seems to be by some use of new critical terminology and awareness, has the kind of visionary ring associated with Mary Daly and Adrienne Rich; it includes the assumption that female experience is somehow locked purely within the women-authored texts and that it will be liberated by a reinvigoration of female fables and myths. Yet many of these myths have been made in the shadow of male constructions; it therefore seems unwise for the study of women's cultural history to exclude any subject-matter and too hurriedly to set boundaries to a search for truth. None the less, it is worth stressing that those who most loudly insist that women's writing is not autonomous and that it shares the conditions of production with men's art often use this notion to concentrate once again on established male-authored texts.

In 1981 Elaine Showalter made a further defensive statement. In 'Feminist Criticism in the Wilderness', an allusion to the earlier deconstructive work of Geoffrey Hartman, she asserted the pluralistic socio-cultural base of American feminist criticism against the charge of its being simply a heterogeneity without norms. But, as in the earlier essay, she found herself occasionally colluding with what she opposed. Although she reasserted her distinction between feminist critique and gynocritics and insisted on the primacy of the latter, she now moved from her earlier antitheoretical stance, while still opposing what she saw as the sterile narcissism of male scholars. She saw her own earlier antitheoretical position as an evolutionary stage and, noting the anxiety in increasingly theoretical English departments at the isolation of feminist criticism, she considered that it did now need a theoretical consensus.

Again there was the call for a feminist criticism that would be genuinely woman-centered, independent and intellectually coherent. But, surprisingly for someone who had recently castigated other deconstructive critics for overdependence on a few dominant men, she turned to the views of two Oxford sociologists, Edwin and Shirley Ardener, who considered women not as inhabitants of separate spheres, as the Victorians seem to have proposed, but as a muted group whose culture and reality overlap with those of the dominant male group; hence women's problems of language and power, for muted groups must mediate their beliefs through the allowable forms of the dominant structures, while also existing in the wild. Women's beliefs find expression through decipherable ritual and art, although there can be no writing entirely outside the dominant structures; the concept of a text wholly in the wild or the wilderness is a playful abstraction. Showalter ended by insisting:

> The first task of a gynocentric criticism must be to plot the precise cultural locus of female literary identity and to describe the forces that intersect an individual woman writer's cultural field. A gynocentric criticism would

also situate women writers with respect to the variables of literary culture such as modes of production and distribution relations of author and audience, relations of high to popular art, and hierarchies of genre (p. 264).

Showalter was arguing more emphatically than before for the socio-historical project of feminist criticism, but there remained problems with her critique. First, her remarks avoided the difficulties of accepting past female literature as transparent to the newly liberated critic; she did not discuss how the confrontation of past text and present reader was to be regulated. Second, her dialectical reliance on Geoffrey Hartman's anterior text, *Criticism in the Wilderness*, as well as her more straightforward reliance on the Ardeners, was odd in the context of her mockery of others who became dubiously kept women by relying on men. The latter reliance was even stranger for being so unnecessary, supporting as it did a commonsensical view she herself seemed to have long held. No one, certainly not Showalter and the Victorian writers with whom she dealt, ever thought that men and women had *nothing* in common. The separate spheres always had some overlap. Third, by still isolating women, even within their muted condition, she seemed to be suggesting an ahistorical enterprise which her own practice belied. Fourth, by making all of male reality accessible to women because it openly becomes the subject of consciousness and legend, while women's extra space is not known to men, women end up again as sole expressers of nature, the wilderness and the female realm. Showalter came close to endorsing the kind of superiority that men for several centuries at least had been all too willing to allow women. Finally, although sniping at it, she did not take on deconstruction directly and so she avoided pointing out its ultimate antagonism to any political statement and any reformist activity: if everything is deconstructible, so are the very words that contain the notion and there is nowhere a position from which to act.[9])

Argument by metaphor

Showalter's debates with critical theory point to a rather bizarre characteristic of her criticism, her habit of arguing through metaphor and simile. It is a ubiquitous tendency, perhaps a reminder of the oral nature of many of the articles she prints, the relics of the many American and British academic conferences that require an established and reliable feminist speaker. Often they have the ring of oral closure, the demand for a burst of laughter which will dispel anything disturbing that might have been implied or said. Or perhaps they allow a disturbing notion to be assimilated without offence. But the habit is less persuasive on the printed page than on the platform.

It may seem churlish to criticize Showalter or anyone else for a liveliness of mind, especially since many of the examples that could be cited are very funny. But the confounding of material through metaphor, playful no doubt in the beginning, occurs so frequently that it becomes real mystification or avoidance.

Many examples could be given. When Showalter is herself convinced but perhaps a little short on argument, she tries to unsettle with laughter and comic image. So following Johnson's Shakespeare into a seductive Cleopatra of an image, she makes feminist criticism's association with men into a 'thrifty feminine making-do', a habit of going round in men's ill fitting hand me downs like the Annie Hall of English studies. In 'Women's Time, Women's Space: Writing the History of Feminist Criticism' (1984), she likens the various 'glittering' theoretical discourses to 'golden apples thrown in Atalanta's path to keep her from winning the race'. The image is immediately striking but it sets up oppositions and contains implications which the article in which it occurs never faces.

The often employed metaphor of criticism as dress is frequently amusing, as it is in 'Criticism in the Wilderness' and in the later 'Critical Cross-Dressing' where it is men who wear feminine attire. The notion of criticism as clothes serves to underline useful points, of the interchangeability of discourses, for example, or of the constructed, fashioned nature of all metacriticism. Yet, with these images, Showalter often escapes from the difficult implications of her genuine arguments against deconstruction and theory.

So too with quick labellings of specific male critics and their theory. A Marxist critic was, for example, described as treading 'those dark alleys of the psyche where Engels feared to tread'. But there are problems with this comic procedure. In *Feminism and Psychoanalysis* (1982) Jane Gallop created a portrait of the psychoanalyst Jacques Lacan within the historical context of Parisian intellectual life; he was so immensely influential on French feminists and so popular with intellectual women that she named him the 'ladies man'. It was a witty sobriquet, but when, in 'Feminist Criticism in the Wilderness', Showalter used it again without context or explanation, she seemed to be foreclosing on a necessary argument with the theory he represented.

Showalter is not alone in this metaphoricity, which can have more baneful epistemological results in less cautious writers. One example has been pointed out by Laurie Finke in her essay 'The Rhetoric of Marginality: Why I Do Feminist Theory' (1986). Noting the ubiquity in feminist scholarship of the image of the margin and marginality, she relates it to the tendency in our patriarchal and Cartesian culture to determine value by hierarchical classification, to assign a name and reify a subject.[10] She sees this tendency manifest in the older type of historical criticism that Showalter represents and she finds it supporting an unthinking opposition to any sort of theory. A kind of dualism of central masculine science and theory on the one side and marginal feminine literature on the other is quickly created which Finke regards as ultimately an essentialist interpretation both of culture and of gender. She takes as an example Jane Marcus's 'Still Practice, A/Wrested Alphabet' (1984), which gives a masculinity to theory by providing it with a body full of muscles; it becomes 'an arrogant apolitical American adolescent with too much muscle and a big mouth' (p. 87).

In my introduction I have already mentioned (and exemplified) the seductiveness of the marginal position for the critic. It is equally seductive – and perhaps more dangerous – as an image of the woman writer. It allows us as modern critics to ascribe to oppression and marginality qualities that have changed in status over the years, instead of facing their existence within an entirely different ideological order, and it helps us to deny an authority that past writings are often asserting but which we are not pleased to acknowledge. So we avoid listening to a past that might be annoying through its resolute refusal to anticipate us.

Perhaps the habit of arguing through metaphor derives partly from the texts on which so many feminist critics work, the women-authored Victorian novels. The narrator of that most exemplary novel for feminist criticism, *Villette*, so flamboyantly rescued by Kate Millett, insisted that the reader compensate for her reticence about her childhood 'through a metaphor'; it is a clever ploy but it rebounds on the narrator whose secrecy, even duplicity, in connection with the major periods and events of her life is made prominent. Lucy Snowe covers her secrecy by urging the reader to create her own image, but imposed images can be just as obfuscating.

All this is not to repudiate arguing through image, but to suggest vigilance and caution. We may end up in the wilderness and on the margins simply because we have situated ourselves there so often.

The anthology

Perhaps nothing so well expresses the mingled authority and uncertainty of present historical feminist criticism in the States as the flight to the anthology, whether it be the Norton anthology of women writers, trying to establish a canon of female literature, or the many anthologies of feminist critical essays. I will mention some recent examples in a later chapter and confine myself here to *The Norton Anthology of Literature by Women* edited by Gilbert and Gubar and *The New Feminist Criticism*, edited by Showalter.

The *Norton Anthology*, published in 1985, aimed to 'recover a long and often neglected literary history' in the words of its compilers. It includes excerpts from women of all periods writing in English, presenting long full texts of works by Kate Chopin, Charlotte Brontë and Toni Morrison. In the twentieth century it shifts its attention decisively from Britain to the USA as if women's writing in Britain more or less stopped when, in the phrase of *1066 and All That*, it was no longer 'top nation.' In Elaine Showalter's words, the anthology aimed to 'establish a feminist canon for the next generation' or, in Gilbert and Gubar's more modest ones, to 'suggest the contours of the canon into which readers will be able to assimilate the works of many other women authors, both those who are writing now and those who have written in the past'.[11]

An immensely useful and simply immense work, the *Norton Anthology* is of great value in allowing those gender connections to be made that have been obscured by more conventional groupings. It skews the great tradition of male literature and suggests a richness where we had long been taught, and are still taught by most general historical anthologies, to expect only poverty. None the less, as an enterprise it becomes just slightly absurd when considered beside Lillian S. Robinson's witty debunking of its footnoting pretensions – errors range from St Francis feeding birds to Napoleon spending his last days on Elba – and her reservations about *any* Norton anthology. Such a work she sees as 'a non-elite packaging of elite content', part of the massification rather than the democratization of higher education. Of more immediate importance to feminist criticism is her warning about the book's assumption that there *is* a female tradition from which a canon can be made.[12]

Perhaps, after all, the whole notion of a canon is dubious. According to Terry Eagleton and Paul Lauter, it is connected with prescriptive critical ideas and the acceptance of a social elite, which the curricula of educational establishments were meant to reinforce.[13] *The Norton Anthology of Literature by Women* is not, however, necessarily destroyed by this objection for, given its aims and subject – the establishment of women – it cannot really include such an idea of the canon. For it is not answering a recognized tradition but making one, and it cannot be said to support a social elite unless it be of the few feminist critics who have achieved status in major academies, hardly a dominant force in the intellectual life of any nation.

But it does seem to me that there is a danger with the *Norton* and that it lies in the other direction. If one subscribes to the idea that a canon is desirable at all or that one is a good idea for pragmatic educational purposes, then its construction for women now seems premature, coming as it does before much empirical and archival work has been done and before the theoretical ideas have been fully addressed by the promoters of women's writing. I have already noted the emphasis in American feminist criticism on the nineteenth century; an anthology that covers all periods cannot of course duplicate this, but, none the less, Gilbert and Gubar can still base their selection on such assertions as: the nineteenth century 'saw . . . the formation, for the first time, of a powerful female literary tradition', giving to women the possibility of intertextuality and revision. But from my reading of the novels of the previous centuries, I would place the beginning of any 'tradition' far earlier. So too with the assertion that throughout the nineteenth century male and female literary traditions were intertwined and interdependent. To some extent, yes, but a version of the eighteenth-century sentimental tradition continues in female fiction and is not noticeably linked with male forms. The *Norton Anthology* is based on the assumptions of its selectors. Perhaps we need to discuss these assumptions before they are Nortonized.

In recent years there have been a spate of anthologies that overlap in their reprinting of a fairly finite number of now established feminist essays, surely making a canon of critical pieces even as we argue about a canon of creative ones. Perhaps this suggests an impasse in feminist criticism or perhaps it indicates a period of taking stock while the future remains unclear and unenvisaged; perhaps it is simply a sensible development since *historical* feminist criticism *should* collect and reassess itself.

Showalter's *The New Feminist Criticism: Essays on women, literature and theory* (1985) is, in its very title, indicative of the progress in American criticism. Where one might expect 'society,' one finds 'theory', but it follows rather than dominates 'literature'. The essays collected, 'new' only in the late 1970s and the early 1980s, hold no surprises. The introduction alone is actually new and it defines the feminist critical revolution in a context less of political feminism than of other critical methods.

In Showalter's view, gender has been established as a fundamental category of literary analysis, and feminist criticism has come of age as a theoretical as well as a practical enterprise. The aim is therefore no longer the exuberant uncovering of misogyny in the Kate Millett manner, but the developing of theories of sexual difference. Deconstruction and other critical methods have, she admits, given much to the language and shifting topics of American feminist criticism, but the influence ought not to be regarded as all one way: 'it now appears that other schools of modern criticism are learning some lessons from our movement, and beginning to question their own origins and directions' (p. 16). In the end, however, she seems to conclude that American feminist criticism and other sorts of critical theory are in their entirety unassimilable by each other.

The language of Showalter's introduction underlines her points. It is often uneasy and eclectic, now speaking formalistically of 'texts', now using an old-fashioned vocabulary of 'literary heritage'. The demanding tone of the 1970s meets the pragmatic one of the 1980s, eliding the theoretical ferment between the two. Theory is accepted and acceptable at one point, while in another a virtue is still made of the lack of authorities; feminist criticism's pluralism is delivered as an avoidance of the reductive single system.

Yet, for all its unease, there is in the introduction as a whole a dignified air of summation. The result of the feminist critical revolution, Showalter argues, has been the opening up of a space 'for the authority of the woman critic that extends beyond the study of women's writing to the reappraisal of the whole body of texts that make up our literary heritage'. It is this 'authority' that Showalter herself most clearly expresses. It is an authority that comes from a certain simple consistency of method. For all her dabbling in translated language, it seems to me that her basic notions have remained constant – even though they sometimes exist beside their own contradictions and even though they are occasionally obscured by the reiterated metaphor. In *The Female Malady* (1985), a study that moved beyond gynocritics to situate women's writing in a complex context of male and female constructions, she continues to argue through image, but in a fairly straightforward, attention-seeking way, while she shows herself acutely aware of the power of repeated metaphors when not brought into consciousness – in this case to determine the definition of women's madness by male psychiatry. Above all she continues her emphasis on past women's writing and her insistence on situating this writing in some form of history.

Without assuming any mystificatory theory and without expecting that anything can be speedily said without some recourse to the academic discourse of investigation, critics like Showalter and Gilbert and Gubar, have retained a mingled academic and general audience. They remain true to the political belief that feminist criticism is not simply a theory among others but that all criticism that does not take in the feminist perspective is flawed and deceiving. They still appear to hold the view – or the utopian hope – that one can come to understand the repression and liberation of an historically constructed culture through the informed study of literature.

Yet it is foolish to conclude too optimistically of the American socio-historical enterprise. For, with all the gains it has made, in the USA at least, the canon of English literature, with its interpretative industry, is pretty much in place in institutions of higher education and the enterprise of academic feminist criticism must always be fragile, situated as it is within an academy largely untouched by its concerns. In the end, then, there is sensible caution in the warnings of Showalter – and many other socio-historical critics – that feminist criticism can join but must not be contained by the polemical circus of theory; it is not another discourse but something that is striving radically to affect and shift all other discourses.

3

French Theory

In the late 1970s American feminist criticism was urgently forced to consider the challenge of French feminist theory, which had been growing in entire indifference to the American enterprise. (I am giving the false impression that deconstruction and psychoanalytical French theory hit the States as discrete successive waves. Perhaps this results from what formalists would see as the narrative urge in my discussion. To a large extent the two movements overlapped and mingled, but there is some difference in dates, and the full force of French psychoanalytical feminist criticism was in the main felt after the shock of deconstruction.) French critics like Julia Kristeva lectured in the USA in the late 1970s and the feminist Hélène Cixous was published in English in the American journal *Signs* in the summer of 1976; in 1980 Elaine Marks and Isabelle de Courtivron compiled their anthology, *New French Feminisms*. A massive inferiority complex was immediately delivered to women who still considered it radical to discover unpublished stories by Kate Chopin or suggest that Sylvia Plath's poems should be in the canon.

Since there were deep distinctions among the French – they ostentatiously attacked each other as scandalous and outrageous – any summary of their views is no doubt intellectually unwise. However, it is possible to say that in the main they united in disapproving of intellectual modes claiming to reveal an empirical reality or an unproblematized history, and they were dubious of any efforts at scrutinizing the surface manifestations of women's oppression; instead the usually hidden body, the unconscious, the deep structures of culture and language, were their data.

Their critique of culture stemmed from a more idealist, less empirical philosophical tradition than the American, one which like deconstruction derived from German phenomenological thinkers. In their project they conversed endlessly with dominant men; using some of the linguistic playful techniques of Derrida and deconstruction, they bounced themselves off the psychoanalytical theories of the Freudian revisionist, Jacques Lacan, who, at this point, made an overwhelming entry into feminist polemics. (The cause of the coupling of Lacan and feminism remains mysterious to me, but it is certainly true that he was in the company of women when he impinged on the Anglo-American consciousness and that it was mainly through feminist criticism that he made his impact in the USA.)

Lacan

For Lacan men and women are only ever in language, language in which gender identities are constantly being composed and decomposed. Language, together with psychological structures, culture and politics, exists within the 'phallic' realm, the order of law, the symbolic. This differs from the imaginary, the pre-oedipal realm where there seems no separation of self and other, mother and infant, a realm that feeds into the unconscious and which is founded on an illusion of wholeness. The speaking subject must exist in language – in the realm of the symbolic therefore – through repressing the (now incestuous) desire of unity with the mother and through accepting the phallus. The phallus is the first mark of sexual difference from the mother, the primary signifier which no one actually possesses, but which none the less seems to have a fairly close relationship with the penis only possessed by men; to speak is to accept the phallus of sexual and linguistic difference and, at the same time, to express the existence of an absence, the repression of desire. Language becomes the substitution for the forbidden mother, for woman, the devalued mother who must be rejected. The desire to be the subject of meaning is the desire to have the other, the mother. But all proofs of love are symbolic and never sufficient; the demand for meaning, significance and love is bottomless: 'Desire is neither the appetite for satisfaction, nor the demand for love, but the difference obtained by subtracting the first from the second,' wrote Lacan in *Ecrits* (p. 691).

While the entry into the symbolic, the realm of the phallus and the law of the father, is an alienation and a separation for both sexes (although to remain in the imaginary too long is to become psychotic), the girl child is especially alienated, since sexual difference is the repressed term that makes the symbolic and its discourse possible. Female desire is repressed and the girl avoids even the clarity of the lack of the phallus experienced by the boy. Lacking even a proper lack so to speak – she has *nothing* to lose – she enters the symbolic with added tentativeness, unable to grasp what has been lost. (In my two-paragraph summary of this notoriously difficult thinker I am no doubt misrepresenting, but my purpose is not to present the complexity of Lacan but to suggest the broad outlines of the Lacan that has been received in the States through French and francophile feminists.)

One might wonder why women sat unyawning through the seminars in which Lacan theatrically propounded this son's drama, this rereading of Freud reading Oedipus. Certainly, he seems to have needed not only woman as the repressed other of symbolic discourse but also women as audience, women as repressed presence for his own discourse to flourish. His stance in his 'seminars' at the Sorbonne has been described by Jane Gallop as that of a cock among the hens, hens who sought to please the teacher rather as the hysterical 'patients' of the nineteenth-century hypnotist Charcot tried to please their master during his public exhibitions or as the Marquis de Sade in prison wanted women to do when he dreamed of their delicious enthrallment to the phallus. But Sade, unlike Lacan, could not, in dream or reality, succeed in making that phallus into a *universal* signifier.

French 'feminists'

Trying to find a route through the apparent eternal and universal patriarchy implied by Lacanian psychoanalysis, French feminists posited an expression uncontrolled by the symbolic. This was *ecriture feminine*, or feminine writing, which would be a utopian projection of repressed femininity, or writing from the body. In various forms and with varying complexity, women such as Irigaray, Kristeva and Cixous spoke of a pre-oedipal, pre-linguistic, pre-symbolic space (Kristeva called it the 'semiotic'), where alone femaleness could be expressed through a mother–infant form of communication before acculturation. It was the place of *jouissance* crudely defined as the re-experiencing of the physical pleasures of infancy before separation from the mother. Ordinary discourse pretended that perception was from a single subject and was immediate and unproblematical. The semiotic space was beyond the subject or the enunciator as traditionally understood and separate from the realm in which political and cultural ideology was inscribed. It was also beyond the passive and conservative imaginary of Lacan and could function as the locus of disruption, displacing the symbolic order where patriarchal language existed and where the male logos was king.

There is perhaps no need to point out that the French critics holding such views had little interest in past female writing which they regarded as deeply embedded within patriarchal cultural and linguistic structures. They were largely uninterested in describing a few markers of how women wrote in distinction to men at a particular unenlightened time in history. The location of such a project would have seemed deeply within the phallocentric realm as an inscribing of the traces of woman, an acceptance of the very power game which had marginalized her in the first place. To examine history was to give it existence, according to Cixous, who looked only to Lacanian psychoanalysis for help. 'Feminism' should be abandoned since the term indicated reformism and its enterprise was deeply compromised by its location within the symbolic realm.

Although French 'feminist' theory had initially been related to the libertarian ferment of 1968, many of its practitioners became increasingly uneasy at any kind of political alignment. They were on the whole uninterested in such mundane and compromising matters as the canon of literature, in limited political aims, or in middle-class academics trying to achieve more classes and find more jobs; the American type of reformist feminism was labelled in post-feminist fashion as dogmatic and political. Kristeva in particular turned from political group activity and, by the late 1970s and early 1980s, having found American capitalism more liberating than Chinese Maoism, she was seeking an answer not in political agitation but in individualistic religious and personal development.

Lacan had seen his writings as mystical and had famously elided psychoanalysis and mysticism in his interpretation of the St Teresa of Bernini as an insatiable orgasmic woman. Avoiding the materialist, Cixous, Irigaray and Kristeva all came close to the mystical in both content and style. In *Speculum of the Other Woman* Irigaray associated women with a non-theological mysticism and with the suffering Christ; in mysticism women experienced a loss of subjecthood which she saw as the only cultural escape in the past from mirrored vision. Cixous, quoting often from the Old Testament, drew on a tradition within Christianity of female attributes of God, expressed in a line of female prophets and messiahs, and her language often resembled the outpourings of, for example, the late eighteenth-century Joanna Southcott, who prophesied a female order in mingled vatic mode of verse and unstructured prose – 'So now the WOMAN see!/ MY CHURCH upon HER it must stand,/ As WOMAN joined with ME'.[1] By the 1980s Kristeva was celebrating the Virgin Mary: '"Her-ethic" is *a-mort, amour. Eia mater, fons amoris*. Let us listen again, therefore, to the *Stabat Mater*, and to the music, all music. It swallows goddesses and strips them of necessity,' words written down two sections of the page in Derridean fashion like the printing of the synoptic gospels.[2]

French theoretical 'feminism' generated in Paris was tied to a particular socio-cultural situation. It consciously manipulated the power of publishing within a small fairly homogeneous society. Its style was French – Kristeva contemptuously referred to 'Anglo-Saxons' – and many of its mannerisms of writing, connected with the gendered language of French, became almost untranslatable into English. None the less, it is worth illustrating in a little more detail the work and style of the three women who had the greatest impact on English-speaking feminists.

Cixous

Hélène Cixous is a dramatist and creative writer who declared that her polemical work should be regarded as poetics rather than general critical theory. Like Derrida, she saw the world as verbal, as text, structured through hierarchical logocentric oppositions, such as culture and nature or activity and passivity, which were founded on gender. Both invoking and seeking to undermine the conventional language of psychoanalysis, which she regarded as representing a masculine view of the world, she separated the female from the male unconscious and regarded the former as the site of the disruption of patriarchal culture. Phallocentrism, the order based on the notion of the phallus as the signifier of power, assumed that the masculine order was conterminous with history itself; an attack on the level of history, the kind of attack that American feminism was mounting, was simply collusive and inappropriate. Only in language was there possibility of disruption and revolution.

'Feminine writing' (the French language makes no distinction between the English 'feminine' and ' female') can exist in women's present and potential creation; indeed women have an especial interest in the disturbance of binary categories that 'feminine writing' enacts. With Kristeva, Cixous was a member of the pro-modernist circle around the journal *Tel Quel* in the 1970s and she found *fémininité* in texts by men like Kleist and Genet, the qualified hero of Millett, as well as by women. Like most of the other French theorists, she regarded a specific concern for writing women of the past as simply an interest in content, 'thematics', which was hopelessly caught in patriarchal assumptions. The texts which she deconstructed or desecrated were usually the philosophical and literary texts by men that Derrida had also privileged. Cixous roundly declared that she was not a 'feminist' in the American sense and she contemptuously defined the term as simply an expression of the bourgeois desire for women's equality in power within the present unchanged patriarchal and late capitalist system.

Cixous was known in the English-speaking world mainly by those texts which were speedily translated, texts which contained her most famous and extreme statements. 'The Laugh of the Medusa' written in French in 1975 and published in English in 1976, is an example; it flaunts its repetitiveness in image and idea with the intention of breaking down the privileged status of the rational published text. It aims to present a surface that cannot be analysed in any systematic, appropriating and male logical way and it celebrates the Derridean notion of *différance*, of meaning not through binary opposition but through process, multiple differentiation that demands no transcendental significance or signified but instead suggests the repressed, unsignified feminine. When the repressed of culture and society returns, Cixous writes, 'it is an explosive, utterly destructive, staggering return, with a force never yet unleashed', a new subverting, life-giving force. Women are urged:

> Write, let no one hold you back, let nothing stop you . . . I write woman:
> woman must write woman . . . Now women return from afar, from
> always: from without, from the heath where witches are kept alive; from
> below, from beyond culture; from their childhood which men have been
> trying desperately to make them forget, condemning it to eternal rest, the

little girls and their ill-mannered bodies immured, well-preserved, intact
unto themselves, in the mirror (p. 227).

This feminine writing or voice, deriving from the mother, is supposed
to arise from the libidinal not the cultural and is produced 'in order to
bring about life, pleasure, not in order to accumulate'. It will not be
theorized, enclosed or coded, surpassing the discourse that regulates
the phallocentric system and 'undoing the work of death'. Such writing
can be produced by men or women and the adjective 'feminine' is
simply shorthand since biological sex is unimportant – although Cixous
finds it rare for men to write in this mode since they have much
investment in the 'phallogocentric' order encoding their supremacy.

Cixous expresses her notions forcibly but her force cannot obscure
the problems. For all her denials, assertions and shiftiness, feminine
writing appears both a particular voluntary mode *and* a biological
possession of women, deriving from the mother. Possibly she is arguing
about representation, not the real, but, even if this is granted, there
seems a slippage as man and woman as signs become man and woman
as physical beings. As Toril Moi puts it in her critique of Cixous in
Sexual/Textual Politics (1985):

> Woman . . . is wholly and physically present in her voice – and writing is
> no more than the extension of this self-identical prolongation of the
> speech act. The voice in each woman, moreover, is not only her own, but
> springs from the deepest layers of her psyche: her own speech becomes
> the echo of the primeval *song* she once heard, the voice the incarnation of
> the 'first voice of love which all women preserve alive . . . in each woman
> sings the first nameless love'. . . . It is, in short, the Voice of the Mother,
> that omnipotent figure that dominates the fantasies of the pre-Oedipal
> baby: 'The Voice, a song before the Law, before the breath . . . was split
> by the symbolic, reappropriated into language under the authority that
> separates. The deepest, most ancient and adorable of visitations' (p.
> 114).

It all sounds much like the traditional glorification of the mother
translated into Derridean and Lacanian French, a step on the way to
post-feminism, the family and woman the nurturer. Cixous prepares
the space, notoriously filling it with mother's milk, the ink of female
writing. Inevitably there are problems of legibility.

Irigaray

More than Cixous, Luce Irigaray, a philosopher and psychoanalyst, celebrated the specifically feminine, at least in its imaginary utopian mode, what could not be written by men. Originally a member of Lacan's *École Freudienne*, she, like Cixous, stayed within a framework of psychoanalysis while coming to disagree with Lacan's conclusions about women, which she felt suggested an unconscious realm governed by the sexual theory of children in which women became men and the mother became merely a function. In a punning, allusive style, which appropriated and deconstructed words and parodied masculine academic discourse, she worked like Derrida to undermine the binary structures of male discourse. She took as her especial target Lacan's notion of the symbolic which she labelled an imaginary, free of historical contingency and universalized into order. The idea of the symbolic relegated women to a state of abandonment and dereliction; in *Ce sexe qui n'en est pas un* (*This Sex Which is Not One*) (1977), Irigaray concluded that 'from a feminine locus nothing can be articulated without a questioning of the symbolic itself' and she asked 'without the exploration of the body/matter of women, what would become of the symbolic process that governs society?' In *Speculum of the Other Woman* (1974) she intended to hold a glass to our conceptions, opposing the male authority expressed in Plato and Freud, whose relationship in time she reversed by beginning with Freud and ending with Plato. Such men dreamed of symmetry through dichotomy, always repressing one term of the masculine–feminine division and making woman subject to the male identity. Woman for Irigaray must exist as a subject herself, as multiplicity. She must be the speaking subject of difference, not simply the opposition or the mirror-image of man.

Although like Cixous she denied bringing psychology and anatomy together, Irigaray in fact asserted the reality of female anatomy against phallocentrism. Women, she felt, were connected to cosmic rhythms and their bodies had an irreducible relation to the universe. She posited a feminine discourse with the structure of the female genitalia, of lips and labia – woman's 'sex is composed of two lips which embrace continually' – denying separation and the dichotomies of self and other. Feminine writing would be rich and creative but not mastering, multiple and in flux, babbling and mimicking; it would be utopian since it could not wholly express and it would be immune from empirical investigation. Above all it would refuse to enact in traditional language and form the male image of woman as the representation of man's desire for reflection of himself. Such writing could and should disrupt, 'If we keep on speaking the same language together, we're going to reproduce the same history'.

In *Reading Woman* Mary Jacobus celebrates the last lyrical chapter of Irigaray's *Ce sexe qui n'en est pas un* as an effort to destroy the unequivocal domination of one mode of signifying over another; it is 'an attempt to release the subtext of female desire, thereby undoing repression and depriving metalanguage of its claim to truth' (p. 77). Fearing any definition of woman as a new essentializing of her and dreading further entrapment in male discourse, Irigaray tries to avoid defining the feminine, which can therefore be read only in the gaps and spaces between signs and in the excess of mimicry. I will quote a fairly lengthy passage to give a taste of the Irigaray style (translated):

[Woman] is indefinitely other in herself. That is undoubtedly the reason she is called temperamental, incomprehensible, perturbed, capricious – not to mention her language in which 'she' goes off in all directions and in which 'he' is unable to discern the coherence of any meaning. Contradictory words seem a little crazy to the logic of reason, and inaudible for him who listens with ready-made grids, a code prepared in advance. In her statements – at least when she dares to speak out – woman retouches herself constantly. She just barely separates from herself some chatter, an exclamation, a half-secret, a sentence left in suspense – When she returns to it, it is only to set out again from another point of pleasure or pain. One must listen to her differently in order to hear an *'other meaning' which is constantly in the process of weaving itself, at the same time ceaselessly embracing words and yet casting them off to avoid becoming fixed, immobilized.* For when 'she' says something, it is already no longer identical to what she means. Moreover, her statements are never identical to anything. Their distinguishing feature is one of contiguity. They touch (*upon*). And when they wander too far from this nearness, she stops and begins again from 'zero': her body-sex organ.

It is therefore useless to trap women into giving an exact definition of what they mean, to make them repeat (themselves) so the meaning will be clear. They are already elsewhere than in this discursive machinery where you claim to take them by surprise. They have turned back within themselves, which does not mean the same thing as 'within yourself.' They do not experience the same interiority that you do and which

perhaps you mistakenly presume they share. 'Within themselves' means
in the privacy of this silent, multiple, diffuse tact. If you ask them insistently
what they are thinking about, they can only reply: nothing. Everything.[3]

I have chosen this particular passage because it has been quoted
several times before and has struck many feminists with its problems.
One is of authority, the positioning of the subject. The American
francophile critic Shoshana Felman, for example, worries about who is
speaking and to whom, as well as about how a woman can be
considered to speak the passage as significance if women cannot speak
meaning at all. To others, such writing seems set deeply within a
framework of patriarchal ideology that, especially from the eighteenth
century onwards, had always provided this irrational space for the
feminine whose unsymbolized condition constantly threatened hysteria. (While I was copying the quotation, I was struck by the dense
use of extratextual devices, italics, quotation marks, and excessive
punctuation, which in the eighteenth century came to be associated
with the gendered writing of 'irrational' women.) Although it may be
labelled mimicry – and it is difficult to see how mimicry moves from
what it mimics – much of Irigaray's writing, avoiding any historical
and materialist analysis, in fact reinforces patriarchal ideology and its
essentialist definitions of women, for, while it purports to question the
sexed language of psychoanalysis, it fails to question its own language
which is deeply embedded in that same psychoanalysis and, while it
postulates a female imaginary, it simply contradicts the male one of
Lacan or at least posits one that has been defined in opposition to the
male.[4] K. K. Ruthven gives a valid if rather smug male response
to the notion: 'It is true that the female "speaking body" is commonly
encountered in the literary tradition, but usually in representations
which most feminists would regard as sexist'.[5] For me the ultimate
problem here is the use of the psychoanalytical framework to
conceptualize social change.

Kristeva

If Irigaray was the heroine of the 1970s, Julia Kristeva is probably the
heroine of francophiles of the 1980s. I have already spoken of her
seductive position of marginality, but there is equal seduction in her

professional status, for in her can truly be found the female intellectual, demanding comparison with Derrida and Lacan. Another seduction for our more passive days may be her stance of nonactivism; her original Bulgarian nationality allowed her to describe a trajectory of sophisticated awareness lacking to Westerners involved in the great awakening of reformist feminism. Indeed, like Cixous, she opposed the 'trap of "feminism"' which she defined as making ourselves into the truth so that we can avoid existing as the unconscious 'truth' of the patriarchal symbolic order.

Like Cixous and Irigaray but with far greater rigour (she was the least fearful of taking on or over the symbolic language), Kristeva stressed the need to transform the subject, that is, to avoid defining the speaking subject as any sort of transcendental ego. Instead she insisted that it was simply a position or a place. Language was a process more than a system, and meaning was contextual and multiple. Language was not simply mimetic, that is, imitating an assumed social reality anterior to it, but itself productive. So any transformation must occur in language. Without this, any apparent transformation in the socio-political realm was absurd. Woman was again associated with the margins and with the pre-oedipal realm of the mother, now existing in the potentially disruptive semiotic rather than in the passive and static imaginary of Lacan, but Kristeva was more hostile to this undifferentiated realm than the celebrating Cixous and Irigaray, seeing it as creatively disruptive certainly but also as dangerous if allowed to overwhelm; woman needed language within the symbolic order to protect herself from the threatened lack of distinction from the mother. So Kristeva spoke openly with what Irigaray tried to deny, authority. The tentative questioning mode disappeared, as well as much of the lyricism, and the voice came from the symbolic – although at the same time Kristeva drew attention to the fraudulence of the enterprise.

Feminine writing or writing in the feminine was for Kristeva, as for Irigaray and Cixous, writing that was not entirely within the symbolic order but writing from the absence, the silences, and incoherence; it was connected with the rhythms and secretions of woman and was described yet again as disruptive, punning, allusive and private. The semiotic, the pre-oedipal babble preceding the symbolic and never entirely repressed in it, formed a kind of incestuous challenge to the symbolic order; it was associated with avant-garde or modernist practice and, although a female modality, it could be produced by male

writers like Artaud and Bataille, as well as by women. Indeed woman
was in this formulation even more than in Cixous's, less a sex than a
stance: 'In "woman" I see somethin that cannot be represented,
something that is not said, something above and beyond nomenclatures and ideologies.'[6] Rather chillingly but more consistently than in
Cixous and Irigaray, feminine writing became in Kristeva's work
simply a stylistic strategy.

Connections and American receptiveness

While the differences in discourse and assumption are obvious – the use
of philosophy, linguistics, psychoanalysis, abstract terminology and
classical and biblical allusion made demands on the reader that would
have been unthinkable in the American context – there are similarities
between French feminists and some radical feminists in the USA such
as Mary Daly or Adrienne Rich. Both rewrite Western narratives, the
one mythological, the other predominantly psychological, and both
dream of a woman's tongue, Rich's common language or Cixous's
another language. Both desire to destroy binary oppositions, including
the fundamental one of male and female and both invoke mythology,
mysticism and the goddess. The basic assumptions of gendered
subjecticity, even the diffused and floating one that deconstruction and
revised psychoanalysis suggest, are similar to the assumptions of
American radical feminism, concerned, unlike Marxist or Socialist
feminism, primarily with sexuality, difference and repression rather
than with material oppression and socio-cultural constraints. Both
valorized female relationships, Rich in the here and now, Irigaray only
when women have remade themselves in the symbolic with language
and rites instead of rivalry.

The political effect is also similar. In 'Power and Danger: Works of a
Common Woman' (1977), Adrienne Rich declared that she found the
word 'revolution' a dead relic of Leftism, part of the deadend of male
politics; instead, like Kristeva, Cixous and Irigaray, she looked to
transformation through language using poetry which concentrates on
the power of language, 'the power of our ultimate relationship to
everything in the universe. It is as if forces we can lay claim to in no
other way, become present to us in sensuous form'. The magical
suggestiveness, the valorizing of poetry, of rune, chant, incantation and

dream, allows expression forbidden anywhere else: 'Think of the deprivation of women living for centuries without a poetry which spoke of women together, of women alone, of women as anything but the fantasies of men. Think of the hunger unnamed and unnameable, the sensations mistranslated' (pp. 248–9). There are traces of socio-historical thinking in Rich and the other American feminists who embraced the notion of women breaking silence and of uncovering themselves, but they share with French feminists the privileging of incantation and suggestiveness.

Yet, despite some similarities to certain strands of American feminist criticism, French theory struck the USA as excitingly alien, especially in its manner and assumptions. The philosophical and psychoanalytical underpinning, the intellectual assurance and the linguistic complexity all seemed novel to women trained in close criticism of texts or in an empirical, mildly historical method of analysis. The impact of the style was felt first by women writing from within departments of modern languages and, then, slowly, by those in English.

Under this influence, the American variety of feminist criticism came to look parochial and naïve. The debate, it was thought, should move from the biologically determined woman to the area of signs and from gender to representation, for it was now understood that, in the words of a critic of French literature, Nancy K. Miller, 'the maxims that pass for the truth of human experience, and the encoding of that experience in literature, are organizations when they are not fantasies, of the dominant culture'.[7] A reading of Freud and Lacan, together with the commentaries of Cixous, Irigaray and Kristeva, seemed a proper step towards the goal of dismantling the theoretical structures in which the feminine was created as a negative term. Feminism and psychoanalysis, as Mary Jacobus argued, became necessary rereadings of each other. An admiring, excited, deconstructing appropriation of Lacan and the 'French' Freud occurred in books and articles that vied with each other in linguistic playfulness and self-consciousness. I will mention only a few critics and their readings, but they must stand in for many more.

Shoshana Felman calls literature the unconscious of psychoanalysis in 'To Open the Question' (1977), while in 'Rereading Femininity' (1981) she glosses Freud's famous question of what is femininity as 'What is femininity for men?' or rather 'What does the question – what is femininity for men? mean for women?'. Felman stresses the need for a notion of sexual difference so that woman will not simply be seen as a mediator of male desire or as a medium of exchange. But gender identity can be travestied or exchanged and so Felman concludes that there is no proper referent for male and female, only the masquerade of masculinity and femininity, a femininity that simply inhabits masculinity as otherness or disruption. Like the French theorists, Felman follows this formalist trajectory right out of reformist feminism as a political philosophy.

Another example of an excitedly Lacanian and self-conscious response came from Jane Gallop in *Feminism and Psychoanalysis: The Daughter's Seduction* (1982). Given its French psychoanalytical orientation, its situation in North America does duty for the necessary marginality, although it tries to make something of the dual heritage – French theory and the 'Anglophone site of this text' – by naming itself a contribution to French psychoanalytical feminist thought 'from the vantage-point of these English-speaking shores'. It is entirely unconcerned with American socio-historical feminism, instead intending to comment pretty exclusively on the relation between French feminist theory and Lacanian psychoanalysis.

Gallop follows Irigaray in making herself into a flexible narrative voice, holding the Lacanian view 'that any identity will necessarily be alien and constraining', but she follows in a way that sometimes sounds like a simple dilution of Irigaray's more extreme position. Her description of her enterprise is that she begins by questioning 'certain feminist assumptions through the agency of Lacanian psychoanalysis' but 'ends by calling into question certain psychoanalytic positions through the agency of feminist writing'. I am not sure that the last part of this description is just and there is, in any case, a revealing change of terms in the formulation that destroys the symmetry. Feminist assumptions – that is, the ground of feminism itself – are said to be questioned by psychoanalysis, while the psychoanalytic *positions*, intentional strategies, are troubled by feminist *writing*. There is more to feminism than writing according to the socio-historical tradition.

Gallop's interpretations oppose Irigaray and Kristeva, although the author in a qualified way admires both. Like other francophile feminists such as Toril Moi, she moves towards the more elitist, 'intellectual' and symbolic Kristeva, although she shares with Irigaray her desire to exhibit phallocracy everywhere, in the hope that another sexual economy might become possible. As in Irigaray, this fixation on phallocracy results in a bizarre fascination for the extremes of patriarchy quite different from the outrage of Kate Millett before the misogyny of Lawrence and Mailer. Here the extreme is inhabited by Lacan and the Marquis de Sade.

The appropriation of Sade, so much a feature of French theoreticians, was already under way when the Surrealist Guillaume Apollinaire called this fantastic torturer of women 'that freest of spirits to have lived so far' and named his manlike heroine Juliette as the woman who would renew the world. The weird appreciation continued with the post-structuralist and psychoanalytic revolutions, in, for example, Barthes and Bataille, and found its way into French feminists and their American followers. But what does Sade actually say in *Juliette*?

Having overturned all other sacred power relationships of subject and ruler or parent and child and having flamboyantly broken the incest taboo that so haunts psychoanalysis, he seems in the tie of two women, Juliette and Clairwil, to be approaching the final reversal of man and woman. Clairwil robustly tells Juliette of her loathing for men: 'I adore revenging my sex for the horrors men subject us to when those brutes have the upper hand'; consequently she and her friend debauch, debase and massacre anything male. But in the end this paragon of a liberated woman declares: 'I live in the name of nothing but the penis sublime; and when it is not in my cunt, nor in my ass, it is so firmly anchored in my thoughts that the day they dissect me it will be found in my brain'. Juliette in her turn is taught to accept not only the penis as obsession but the phallus as a religion: 'This too,' says her master pointing to his penis, 'is my god, let it be one unto thee, Juliette: extol it, worship it, this despotic engine, show it every reverence, it is a thing proud of its glory, insatiate, a tyrant . . .'.[8] And she agrees. Sade has trampled on all social inhibitions and ties, mocked duty to God, parents and children and all hierarchies of virtue and age, but he does not fantasize the ultimate revolution of women against men.

Mary Jacobus is more concerned with English than with French literature but her approach has much in common with Gallop's. In *Reading Woman* she summed up her enterprise in the following way:

> literature turns from experience to psychoanalysis for an answer to the riddle of femininity, [and] psychoanalysis turns the question back to literature, since it is in language – in reading and in writing woman – that femininity at once discloses and discomposes itself, endlessly

displacing the fixity of gender identity by the play of difference and vision which simultaneously creates and uncreates gender, identity, and meaning. 'The difference (of view)' which we look for in reading woman (reading) is surely nothing other than this disclosure, this discomposition, which puts the institution of difference in question without erasing the question of difference itself (p. 24).

An example of the approach is her discussion of the ending of George Eliot's *Mill on the Floss*, a text much analysed by socio-historical critics.

This ending in which the heroine and her brother are drowned together has struck many readers as awkward and unsatisfactory. The earliest enthusiastic phase of feminist criticism had difficulty assimilating it into a pattern of exemplary female history; the next, gynocritics, can be indicated by Showalter's *A Literature of Their Own* which placed the book in the feminine stage of the novel's development and declared of the ending, 'Maggie never penetrates to the depths of her own pain; she diverts all her energy into escape and self-stupefaction. The ultimate flood is lethal, it seems, because the heart's need has been dammed up for so long' (p. 129). Showalter's description of Maggie's evasion of responsibility allowed Eliot also to evade responsibility for an ending which became a reflection of Victorian feminine turmoil in general.

When Mary Jacobus attends to the ending she sees metaphor made real. The heroine lives and dies by the conventional morality of female suffering, so that the author herself can release a flood of desire that is language. In this reading the book becomes a kind of ur-Irigaray in which both modern critic and Victorian novelist happily kill off the woman engulfed in masculine language and logic and both end by releasing, as she sinks, 'a swirl of possibility'. This degree of emphasis on language seems here to verge on misappropriation.

American scepticism

Despite widespread enthusiasm for things French, there were many disgruntled diggers in literature who regarded the new theory as an unnecessary, indeed obstructive, mystification of woman, while the language in which it was delivered appeared at times a howling psychobabble.

As I have suggested already, some American critics , harking back to the earliest phase of feminist criticism, simply opposed all theory, whether supplied by feminism, deconstruction or psychoanalysis. Others lamented the extraordinary polarizations of discourses which the adoption of French methods and terminology brought with it and the consequent lack of any common framework for debate. It seemed that no judgements of plausibility or persuasiveness could really be made across theory lines.

But a few made specific rejoinders. In 'Feminist Criticism in the Wilderness,' Showalter refused to find a useful theory in the new French feminist psychoanalytical criticism, which she scorned for being based upon phallic and ovarian theories of art. Anatomy simply became textuality in a criticism which depended on a male-centered, reductive and ahistorical psychoanalysis. Showalter mocked the linguistic theories of French feminists for their advocacy of a revolutionary break from dictatorial and patriarchal speech, since she saw this idea as yet another eruption of the primarily male myth of women's secret place and language.

A less abusive and more sustained assessment came from Ann Rosalind Jones in an article entitled 'Writing the Body: Toward an Understanding of l'Ecriture feminine' (1981). She questioned both the theoretical consistency of French feminism and the practical and political implications of its celebration of the feminine. Worrying about the basic assumption that women could experience their bodies and their sexuality outside 'the damaging acculturation so sharply analyzed by women in France and elsewhere', she pointed to the acceptance by most thinkers of the idea that early gender identity comes into being in response to patriarchal structures; there can then be no essential stratum of sexuality unsaturated with social arrangements and symbolic systems. The French feminists, Jones argued, 'make of the female body too unproblematically pleasurable and totalized an entity'. Behind Cixous's glorification of the drive towards gestation she heard echoes of the 'coercive glorification of motherhood that has plagued women for centuries'. With many opponents of this thinking, she points out its genesis in those very symmetrical oppositions of the ideological system feminists want to destroy. Certain kinds of French feminism simply reversed values but left the man as the determining referent. Why stay in binary logic at all?

Although Jones did not mount an entire attack on the stylistic habits of the proponents of Lacan and '*écriture feminine*', she did note that their discourse, with its puns, neologisms, and playfulness, needed 'a thoroughgoing familiarity with *male* figureheads of Western culture'. Only with such a background could a reader recognize the intertextual game being played. The work of these theoretical writers showed that a resistance to culture was always built, at first, of bits and pieces of that culture, however disassembled and criticized.

In a later article 'Julia Kristeva on Femininity: The Limits of a Semiotic Politics' (1984), Jones focuses on Kristeva. The existence of the symbiotic symbolic and semiotic realms in Kristeva's thinking allowed the social to be associated with the former and so to be both constant and ever repressive. The only rupturing is not in political activity, which is pointless since the social world is structurally immutable but in literary discourse. Woman becomes (productively) marginal and motherly again and there is no interest in women specifically as writers or as agents of change and culture. In fact there seems little possibility of women as agents at all. Kristeva herself, however, seems free of this logic. Claiming marginality, she sits at the centre of power and symbolic language, arguing that for a woman to assume power is to introduce a crack in representation; the only route forward is to exercise power and simultaneously criticize it. At other times, however, she dreams the Irigarayan dream of a woman as a unique being capable of the 'impossible dialectic of two terms'.

Jones considers that French theory was stimulating in the USA at a moment when the initial feminist excitement for political causes had waned or had been subdued. The Equal Rights Amendment was defeated and the backlash of the moral majority was being expressed in the media. French psychoanalysis, both Lacanian and revised Lacanian, was a coherent intellectual theory; its discourse was difficult to understand and use and immersion in it seemed in some ways a substitute for the external activity that many feminist critics in the earlier less sophisticated years felt should accompany academic effort. This seems to me a fair assessment.

4
Confrontations

I have mentioned a few studies critical of French theory, as well as one or two interventions in its mode. More effort, however, went into two other projects. The first was a struggle to effect a reconciliation between the French theory and American socio-historical criticism; the second was an attempt to discredit the latter altogether as old-fashioned and hopelessly naïve.

Reconciliations

There was no easy synthesis possible but an effort at reconciliation in practice occurred in some books by younger scholars who found a compromise through a less populist criticism than that produced by 1970s feminism. They aimed to combine formalist, psychoanalytical and historical, Marxist and feminist, gynocritics and the female critique, and they looked at literature and culture as a source of repression and dispersal of femininity. The female relationship to cultural structures came to the fore and the concept of gender replaced the concept of woman. The new developments may be discerned in a series from the University of Chicago Press, *Women in Culture and Society*, presented by Catherine Stimpson; it includes works such as Mary Poovey's *The Proper Lady and the Woman Writer: Ideology as Style in the Works of Mary Wollstonecraft, Mary Shelley, and Jane Austen* (1984), Ellen Pollak's *The Poetics of Sexual Myth, Gender and Ideology in the Verse of Swift and Pope* (1985), and Margaret Homans's *Bearing the Word: Language and Female Experience in Nineteenth-Century Women's Writing* (1986).

All three of these books seek to uncover the strategies from accommodation to subversion that women (and men) indulge in when confronted with the myths, bourgeois, Romantic or psychoanalytical, of patriarchal culture; they all try to uncover the assumptions of discourses, general bourgeois, medical, legal or literary. They all reveal a sometimes reductive, sometimes sophisticated and illuminating use of psychoanalytical theories yoked to a varying concept of ideology. Instead of reaching towards posthumous psychoanalysis of an author, as an old-fashioned psychological criticism might have done, they insist that analysis should be of the writing and of the relationship of writing to the imperatives of gender in the culture. The aim, typical of the newer kind of critics, is, then, textual and ideological, formalist in the sense that works are viewed as verbal structures, but going beyond formalism in the desire to prove that questions of intrinsic and extrinsic, text and context, ultimately converge. The hope is, as Ellen Pollak well expresses it, to unite formal and sociopolitical concerns so as to avoid the ahistorical danger in deconstruction and the naïve view of empirical neutrality in historical criticism. Since I will be returning to Poovey in the final section on Mary Wollstonecraft, I will illustrate the mode more fully from Homans, whose book Stimpson describes as a 'major work of literary theory'.

Calling on the Freudian revision of Nancy Chodorow, *Bearing the Word* purports to study the Lacanian story as cultural myth, one that has inherited the quest story of the Romantic poets, for in psychoanalysis the Romantic 'Mother Nature' has become Lacan's lost maternal presence. In the myth, the male poet rejects the mother and the pre-oedipal realm by entering the symbolic and language and by accepting women as matter or nature. For him, language is constructed through the death or absence of the mother and the quest on which he embarks is seen as a quest for a substitution which will work the transference of maternal power onto something more controllable by men. The problem then arises about what happens to a woman writer.

When *she* enters the symbolic order of language, she has more trouble participating in it as a subject because of the constant objectifying of the feminine within the culture in which she exists. Yet, she has compensations for this difficult state of affairs, since a daughter – who herself will be a mother – remains less frightened of identifying with the mother than a son and will, therefore, in the end be capable of two languages, the literal maternal one which the man has lost and the figurative symbolic one of the patriarchal order. Nineteenth-century women writers, in Homans's argument, attempt to reclaim their own experiences as paradigms for writing; they experiment with a literary practice that would value women as literal – that is, connected with motherhood as daughters and mothers rather than connected solely with the signifying penis. But the literary practice is limited by the fact that patriarchal culture controls the construction of the mother.

In her foreword to Homans's study, Catherine Stimpson claims that the argument is not 'crude biological' determinism. Certainly it is not 'crude' – like most of the francophile feminist critics, Homans writes with great subtlety and self-awareness, raising (though not always answering) objections which are usually left to readers in less self-conscious works. Yet there does in fact appear a certain biological determinism, owing to a muddling of physical and metaphorical, the slippage, reminiscent of Cixous, from metaphysical to material. The idea that women are associated in some cultural myths with the 'literal' imperceptibly in Homans's book becomes their actual linguistic situation. Such slippage easily allows rather dubious historical or material statements, for example, that subordination becomes a privilege. It may, I suppose, have compensations but I am wary of anything that so usefully transforms a disadvantage. There is too a sense of determinism conveyed by the method of arguing; the grid of modern psychoanalysis is placed on women, and individual experience becomes universal drama. The Lacanian story stands in for history.

Stimpson praises Homans for the way she lays bare the complexities and complicities of the female ambition to bear the word as well as the child. I am not sure that the two can in any way be brought together, let alone equated. What is more obviously laid bare is not the parallel bearing of children and books but another parallel, of psychoanalytical and poetic myths, both of which obscure a shifting and specific history. The experience of motherhood is not, after all, timeless; to treat it as if it were so is to risk locating women in another (Romantic) margin. It is a dubious (as well as smug) assertion, based on the Romantic male myth which it seems to deny, that women cannot write the Immortality Ode because, unlike men, they lose nothing in maturing (Dorothy Richardson) or that they need not do so because they retain the mother (Homans).

Homans is obviously somewhat uneasy at her enterprise for, towards the beginning of her book, she asserts:

> There is all the difference in the world between countless nineteenth- and many twentieth-century 'experts' telling women that wifehood and

motherhood is their proper sphere and proper duty . . . and recent
studies by female and feminist psychologists, philosophers, and other
scholars concerning both the origins and the genuinely positive value, for
men as well as women, of such traditional female roles as child rearing
and such traditional female values as pacifism. This is scholarship that
would restore women's difference to women's own – and probably quite
novel – uses. To study gender difference from a woman's perspective is to
begin to redress the appropriation of women's lives by androcentric
culture (p. 28).

I doubt that there is 'all the difference in the world' – 'difference' is a
slippery word, like 'novel' – and I suspect that 'experts' and
psychologists are much of a muchness.

The books in the *Women in Culture and Society* series represent an
appealing intellectual project of synthesis. But they lack the exciting
breadth of reference of the earlier, more accessible criticism of Moers or
Ellman and the historical specificity of Showalter. Although Homans
claims to be attending to uncanonical texts, her authors are the usual
Greats of nineteenth-century literature, especially Eliot and Gaskell,
while Poovey stays with Mary Wollstonecraft, Mary Shelley and Jane
Austen (Pollak's corpus is a a few poems of Pope and Swift). There is
no reason why a critic should refer widely, but, in the case of the
women writers who have so often been seen in isolation from their
contemporary sisters, the procedure does reinforce both their historical
atypicality and their links with what is fast becoming a Great (female)
Tradition through their participation in the dramas of (Chodorovian)
Lacan. Although Homans is aware of her 'melioristic phrasing', she
does seem to hold a progressive notion of this tradition, making of
Virginia Woolf, for example, a bolder version of the nineteenth-century
writer (the usual francophile valorizing of modernism). In addition, in
the sort of criticism that aims to use both socio-historical scholarship
and psychoanalysis, genres in their historical manifestations may
become blurred. In Homans, for example, fiction and non-fictional
works fall together, and the maternal diary of Gaskell yields much the
same as the novels in which she struggled to enter the public and
professional world. In short, I find this sort of criticism, acute and
stimulating though it frequently is, too eager to downplay the
specificities of past culture and past literature, as well as too willing to
privilege theory and the psychoanalytical explanation. The reader and
the present are brought to the fore and any seemingly inappropriate

respect for the author is silenced. Her perhaps tentative efforts to communicate become a resistible authority of the text and her intervention in the public world and culture simply an expression of the constraints and benefits of being a woman.

I want now to consider the direct attack made on the American type of historical criticism from the standpoint of French-inspired theory. I will concentrate on Toril Moi, Mary Jacobus and Alice Jardine whose work seems to me to present the most sustained critique.

Toril Moi

Sexual/Textual Politics (1985), an introductory summary by Toril Moi, is advertised as exposing 'the strengths and limitations of the two main strands in feminist criticism, the Anglo-American and the French'. In fact, however, the book mainly attacks American socio-historical criticism from inside European institutions and it takes its (critical) standpoint largely from French theory and psychoanalysis. It refers constantly to *Anglo*-American feminist criticism, although no British women are discussed and its use of the term as intellectual tradition rather than geographical location suggests the heady divorce of the analysis from time and place.

Beginning ringingly with the statement that 'the principal objective of feminist criticism has always been political', it criticizes most harshly precisely that line of enquiry that has, with considerable faltering, tried to hold to this goal. While ultimately keeping her own position obscure, Moi privileges the writing of French theorists, especially Kristeva – placed last in this ahistorical study – who is arguably the most apolitical and anti-feminist of the theoreticians. Her long final quotation is given to Derrida and his sybilline 'dream' of a utopia beyond the binary opposition of masculine and feminine. Well, it is a good dream, but perhaps it does not at this stage encompass the feminist temporal and reformist project.

Moi finds absurd the fear expressed by critics such as Showalter that emphasis on theory will obscure women's writings, since everything is, in her view, theorized in the first place. She is harsh on the naïvety of early American work of the Showalter and Gilbert and Gubar sort, which she accuses of fearing the text and avoiding the proper 'hermeneutics of suspicion'. In *The Madwoman in the Attic*, Moi finds a lamentable belief in a '*real* woman hidden behind the patriarchal textual facade' (p. 61), who can be discovered through assiduous criticism. Not having read Barthes carefully before they began, Gilbert and Gubar erroneously accept the authority of the female author whom they see as a unified self composing a text which is an organic whole. The critics are caught within the traditional aesthetic values of patriarchal and humanist criticism, preferring realism to modernism and autocratically telling a story of all women.

Showalter shares the faults of Gilbert and Gubar and adds others. Within her criticism, Moi charges, there is the assumption that writing should be an expression of personal experience in a social context. Like Gilbert and Gubar, she favours nineteenth-century realistic writing that assumes a representational, mimetic relationship to the society in which it occurs. Trapped in this pre-modernist world, she too adheres to the concept of the unitary self, a hopelessly unfashionable position which props up the critical edifice of such unreconstructed Marxists as Georg Lukács. But, in an unkind turn, Showalter is made the outcast of all schemes, since she is not only a reactionary realist but also a devotee of 'traditional bourgeois humanism of a liberal-individualistic kind' (p. 6). She is accused of not being a Marxist revolutionary but only a feminist. Showalter's failure is exemplified in her uneasiness with the feminist writings of Virginia Woolf, especially *A Room of One's Own*, the Derridean, Freudian resonances of which she cannot appreciate. The American critic, exemplar of the whole approach of American feminist criticism, demands a simple realism and is 'incapable of appropriating for feminism the work of the greatest British woman writer of this century [Virginia Woolf]' (p. 8).

This seems rather unfair. Showalter's point was surely not that writers *should* write in a particular way, but that the critic should ask for some awareness in the writer; an upper middle-class woman could know that she is writing from that position. I have already alluded to the effects of Showalter's privileging of Victorian literature, a mark of the early phase of feminist criticism in general, but, having agreed with Moi's point concerning the favouritism, I would not want to fall into a favouring of modernism or into allowing these 'isms' to do duty for evaluative adjectives – for modernism read revolutionary, for bourgeois realism read reactionary. The 'revolutionary' doctrine has landed Kristeva in mystification, exhibitionist psychoanalysis and quietism; although Moi is coy about heroines – she has mocked early feminism for its childish liking for them – yet, if a heroine must be found in her text, it is surely Kristeva.

Perhaps Moi's high assessment of Woolf is just, but could we not consider it all a little more before moving into the Leavisite mode of absolute assertion? For a critic who mocks the American propensity to set up a new women's canon, such assertiveness is strange indeed. And the Woolf that Toril Moi delivers by way of Kristevan psychoanalytical metaphysics is hardly more convincing than Showalter's. Woolf becomes a woman who has let the semiotic disrupt the symbolic order; so she runs the risk of madness since, if the 'unconscious pulsations were to take over the subject entirely, the subject would fall back into pre-Oedipal or imaginary chaos and develop some form of mental illness'. Woolf's mental illness 'can be linked both to her textual strategies and to her feminism' (p. 11). The combining of femininity, feminism and madness hardly forms a revolutionary suggestion.

While I think it is much too harsh in its strictures on American feminist criticism, Moi's book is useful for its isolation of a universalizing tendency in this socio-historical project, its historical rather than psychoanalytical telling of the story of all women (the tendency is repeated in the synthesizing works of Homans and Poovey). But, in the earlier criticism, it did at least remain at the level of story – its fictional nature was clear – and so there was room for change. Although Moi assumes that this story is an Aristotelian one with beginning, middle and end, a unified story of the 'Great Mother Writer', this need not be so; instead it can be seen as episodic, serialized or multiple – there may be as many stories as one wants. Gilbert and Gubar's story is simply an example, one that is in my view too little aware of history, but it is not therefore patriarchal or revisionary. It is only when the story is the psychoanalytical one that it risks endless repetition.

Moi argues that, in American criticism, history or the text simply becomes the expression of a unique individual; all art turns into autobiography and becomes a mere window onto the self and the world, with no reality of its own. 'The text is reduced to a passive, "feminine" reflection of an unproblematically "given", "masculine" world or self' (p. 8). Well why? Are history and the text interchangeable? Why is looking at the self necessarily looking at the world and why is the autobiographical necessarily the socially realistic? Why, above all, must we accept the connection of feminine and passive, feminine and reflection, masculine and the world? Is this a self-aware parody of such dualistic thinking or a reassertion of it? For a work that takes pains to expose the assumptions of other works, there seems an immense amount assumed here.

Mary Jacobus

Mary Jacobus's book *Reading Woman* takes a stand firmly on the necessity of French influence on American feminist criticism and she sees this influence as a stage on the path towards feminist maturation. 'It is scarcely possible to write feminist literary criticism in the 1980s without acknowledging the influence of French or Franco-feminist critics, theorists and mediators.' She dates the influence of French literary theory on untheoretical gynocritics from the mid- to late 1970s. Not intending to be a survey like Moi's *Sexual/Textual Politics*, Jacobus's book with its emphasis on early American feminist criticism seems somewhat anachronistic. This appearance is strengthened by its use of old articles that repeat the battle lines of the years in which they were originally written.

Reading Woman makes a direct attack on feminist literary history in the persons of 'herstorians'. These are the by now much maligned interpreters of the 1970s like Showalter and Gilbert and Gubar, 'untheorized, experiential, and literary-herstorical', stuck blindly in the mode of literary masculinity. Jacobus labels them 'essentialist', that necessary term of abuse in feminist critical vocabulary. Especially disliking Showalter's concentration on female writing, she disputes the idea that women writers should be privileged in criticism since the category of woman writer is inevitably problematic itself and since an intervention of psychoanalysis is needed to show how 'difference' is produced. Only through psychoanalysis can women's writing be freed from the determinism of origin or essence, which is reiterated not probed in the herstory approach.

Jacobus exemplifies Showalter's critical muddle by the piece on critical cross-dressing where, Jacobus argues, she allows female impersonation and reading as a woman to become elided; instead of following her perceptions into psychoanalysis, Showalter retreats into the experience of being female – always anathema to Jacobus; she is punished by being psychoanalysed herself and revealed as a slightly puritanical figure who worries about going too far.

Gilbert and Gubar are judged as limited by a theory of gender in which the relation between the body and the subject remains unmediated by the unconscious and by language. If one follows the Gilbert and Gubar line, Jacobus argues, women will always be discovered as madwomen in the attic since, in this view, literary history is a conspiracy to marginalize or repress them. To lack theory is to accept the truth of gender for 'the very notion of (literary) history attempts to repress ambiguity and division; and what is repressed necessarily returns, in the language of the unconscious, as an avenging monster' (p. 9). In other words the disorders of history are used by Gilbert and Gubar to fix the threatening disorders of gender identity.

Although Jacobus, like Homans, defuses criticism by anticipating it, none the less it may still be observed that her account seems uncomfortably and uncompromisingly ahistorical. Her practice is prepared for by her book's method; it is a collection of past essays, the dates of which can only be discovered through the acknowledgements. Yet she mentions in her preface her own trajectory towards French psychoanalytical criticism; does history stop at conversion? Certainly theory seems to stop with Lacan, who may be reinterpreted, with ever increasing subtlety but never ignored, for the Lacanian theoretical model appears to have a supra-historical validity which prevents Jacobus from historicizing her own practice and stance, as well as Lacan's.

If, as Jacobus argues in *Reading Woman*, the approach exemplified by American herstorians is essentialist, it appears to me that hers is idealist. Everything becomes representation and difference. Yet the images and language that are deconstructed in her essays are historically real, however false they may appear to late twentieth-century readers. Something may be true historically, perhaps not so essentially, and remain the object of study. To criticize from the standpoint of a feminine writing or the point of disruption and excess alone is ultimately to refuse intelligibility and to reinscribe femininity in excess and derangement, more completely and hopelessly than Gilbert and Gubar could ever have done.

Apparently it is impossible to accept the franco-based opposition to historical criticism in any large measure without some acceptance of Lacan and Freud, battered and reinterpreted undoubtedly, but still absolutely present, along with their inevitably male universal subject – male regardless of whether or not 'male' and 'female' are simply signifiers. Critics like Jacobus influenced by Lacan may argue that women need not necessarily and totally be trapped in a masculine discourse, but they start with a monolith which creates an opposition which both complicates and simplifies their endeavour.

The result seems endless searching for utopian (semiotic) writing, which concentrates attention only on modernist experimentation or its foreshadowings in the ruptures and fissures of a few canonical past texts. The long tradition of actual female writing which it has been the business of American historical feminist criticism to recover is ignored. The concentration on women's writing that cannot be written wipes out any concern for what can and has. French-influenced critics like Jacobus make no effort to remake or shake the canon, and it appears that theory can substitute for reading female writers of the past; 'reading woman' takes over from reading women.

Alice Jardine

In 'Gynesis' (1982) and *Gynesis* (1985), article and book, Alice Jardine follows Moi and Jacobus in taking issue with American feminist criticism. However, she avoids the condescending tone of Moi and the slightly doctrinaire one of Jacobus who was, admittedly, writing her essays in times that were less open than Jardine finds them to her theory and critique.

Jardine makes herself a kind of returned exile. She has flirted long and hard with French theory but has come home to the States unmarried. None the less, whatever her declared status, she is immensely involved with the theory she deconstructs, and her irritation with the simplistic ways of her compatriots is as great, if not as directly expressed, as that of the foreigners Moi and Jardine. Fully aware how dependent are the French women, Cixous, Irigaray and Kristeva, on male theory and men-authored creative texts, she still relies on them to shape her questions.

Like Jacobus, Alice Jardine accuses American historical criticism of having a naïve empirical view of reality, of failing to understand that '"Truth" and "reality" are . . . radically and irrevocably problematized.' This criticism has also failed to grasp that it is not the self, a woman or a man, that speaks but 'language, the unconscious, the textuality of the text': the 'assurance of an author's sex within the whirlpool of decentering is problematized beyond recognition . . .' (p. 57). 'The question of whether a "man" or "woman" wrote a text (a game feminists know well at the level of literary history) is nonsensical.' The 'commonsensical' view, the literary historian's notion of an author, is ridiculed as the very humanism that feminism is trying to undermine, while the interest in signature, the basis of gynocritics, seems the last infirmity of the feminist critical mind.

Opposing gynocritics, gynesis subverts the anachronistic dichotomies of man and woman on which such criticism is based. Gynesis is related to 'the breakdown of the conscious, Cartesian Subject, the default of Representation, and the demise of Man's truth' (p. 27), the deconstruction of what Meaghan Morris has called the 'Big Dichotomies'; it is the 'putting into discourse of "woman" as that *process* diagnosed in France as intrinsic to the condition of modernity; indeed, the valorization of the feminine, woman, and her obligatory, that is, historical connotations, as somehow intrinsic to new and necessary modes of thinking, writing, speaking. The object produced by this process is neither a person nor a thing, but a horizon . . . a reading effect, a woman-in-effect that is never stable and has no identity' (p. 25).

According to Jardine, the flaw in American gynocritics is its reliance on pre-modernist notions of subject experience and representation. This reliance results in a lack of theory and a reactionary praxis, while old ways of thought and knowledge are left in place. Instead of reiterating falsities, cataloguing and explicating texts, we should be putting texts in dialogue with each other, laying bare the vicious circles of liberal and humanist ideology, based on reified and naturalized categories like experience and the natural, and denaturalizing the world. We must read 'symptomatically (metaphorically)' although somehow the primary question should remain 'metonymical: what can possibly come next?'.

Jardine's analysis has much in common with Jacobus's, at least in what it opposes. And so some of the same defence may be suggested. Truth and reality have indeed been problematized and only a few of the older academic establishments of Britain could doubt it. None the less the problem of representation remains, its absolute foregrounding at the expense of the material. Truth may admittedly be man's truth but I question whether reality can be so clearly assigned.

To read symptomatically is obviously an immense gain over the naïve reading that failed to grasp the anxieties and tensions in a text, as well as those similar qualities in the reader. But to read texts *only* symptomatically is to find in them only symptoms of present systems of thought. The symptomatic reading of texts can cause a refusal to learn of and from the alienating effect of other modes. Deconstruction not based on an understanding of the construction in time, can surely be simply destructive. Privileging the metaphorical, the spatial, and the synchronic, Jardine seems to assume that the diachronic will take care of itself and yet she expects or hopes that a future will simply emerge from the present.

Jardine is concerned solely with modernist and post-modernist literature and with the 'crisis of modernity' which she accuses American socio-historical criticism of failing to assimilate. But this exclusivity seems to me as limiting as American criticism's emphasis on the nineteenth century. Irigaray sees in modernism the speculative object speaking, but this formulation will not do for women writers of earlier periods. These women would of course be dismissed as writing deeply within patriarchy; yet it would seem wise to listen to their voices, however mediated, translated or metamorphosed, to see whether our assumptions about the power and effect of patriarchy hold, to hear what the Big Dichotomies can do before they are (if they are) shaken by us. Is it not possible that Jardine's formulations take the form they do because they come solely from modernism? As she quotes Geoffrey Hartman as saying, 'every literary theory is based on the experience of a limited canon or generalized strongly from a particular text/milieu'.[1] It seems that literature as well as history is taken as read or not read. But to take it so is to have it all the men's way, for the periodizations of the past and the canon emerging from the past have come from men alone. The present is made of concepts formulated in the past when man, with the logos, was king.

Gynesis is an attractive because somewhat vertiginous book which, in the end, I feel should be resisted, not for any puritanical refusal of its pleasure, but because I am decidedly unprepared to exchange the concept of 'women' for the 'woman-effect'. Feminism inevitably dies in the exchange since, if there is no woman in the representations of history, only representation itself, then there is no one to liberate. Feminism as simply the complex play of humanist ideology is obviously no feminism at all and it can easily be dematerialized into an anachronism. And yet there are women still; they do not get jobs because they are women, they raise children alone because they are women, and they write out of the same indestructible fact. 'Not believing in "Truth", we continue to be fascinated by (elaborate) fictions,' writes Jardine. 'This is the profound paradox of the feminist speaking in our contemporary culture: she proceeds from a *belief* in a world from which – even the philosophers admit – *Truth* has disappeared' (p. 31). *Even? Admit?* Perhaps it depends on what truth. Patriarchy, bread, pain? Because there is no Universal Truth it does not mean there is no truth at all.

Images and questions

As I have argued, the socio-historical criticism exemplified by Showalter was much given to metaphor and simile. Troping – but at a far less superficial, intermittent and dramatic level – is also the mode of francophile writing and it arrives with deep significance from Lacanian psychoanalysis.

In Lacan's scheme, language is 'male' because it is based on the lack of the maternal. It is the figurative substitute in the symbolic order of the physical maternal body in the pre-oedipal. Metaphoric language is thus associated with male control, and women form the suppressed other, the literal, the absent referent which facilitates the figurative language of men. Yet if women do use metaphoric language, they can disrupt this male control. Something of this notion must be behind the extraordinary style of punning, metaphor, playful etymologizing and word vertigo adopted by many of the psychoanalytical critics. Argument is born from the accidents of language, the pun, both in the criticism and in the texts that are scrutinized. Since there is no concept of authorial intention, the text can lurch into meanings through odd changes in a word's significance and can reveal its own unconscious by unexpected conjunctions. Word play becomes the secret of the text and a method of criticism.

Mary Jacobus quotes a passage from George Eliot's *The Mill on the Floss*:

It is astonishing what a different result one gets by changing the metaphor! Once call the brain an intellectual stomach, and one's ingenious conception of the classics and geometry as ploughs and harrows seems to settle nothing. But then, it is open to some one else to follow great authorities and call the mind a sheet of white paper or a mirror, in which case one's knowledge of the digestive process becomes quite irrelevant. It was doubtless an ingenious idea to call the camel the ship of the desert, but it would hardly lead one far in training that useful beast. O Aristotle! if you had had the advantage of being 'the freshest modern' instead of the greatest ancient, would you not have mingled your praise of metaphorical speech as a sign of high intelligence, with a lamentation that intelligence so rarely shows itself in speech without metaphor, – that we can so seldom declare what a thing is, except by saying it is something else?

Jacobus notices the self-congratulation lurking in the passage, the manner in which Aristotle loses his authority to the author herself. Despite its apparent emphasis on empiricism as the order of the day, she see it, partly in its choice of hackneyed images, as recognizing on some level that language is endlessly duplicitous and metaphor; a kind of exciting impropriety or 'oxymoronic otherness' (p. 74).

Like all Jacobus's readings this is an ingenious one, but I think it slurs over the main point by casting an inevitable slur on empiricism. Duplicity is energizing ambiguity perhaps, but it is first and foremost deceit and the result of the image here cannot be entirely accounted for in her way. Also, the camel as ship of the desert is indeed a hackneyed image as she notes, but it is the more powerful because it is so. New and striking metaphor may well be an instrument of knowledge; the hackneyed metaphor that has come to do duty for the world out there surely constricts it. Its danger is that it can become partial and reductive truth.

Despite the inventive playfulness in the psychoanalytical criticism, certain metaphors or tropes recur to the point where they are as hackneyed as – and more dangerous than – Eliot's ship of the desert, or indeed Showalter's very obvious critical clothes. One example is the catachrestic image of the text as a body. This has been a feature of much modern criticism, such as that influenced by the French historian–philosopher, Michel Foucault, whose followers tend to find the human body repetitively mutilated in the most disparate places. In feminist criticism it becomes sexualized. So Jacobus can 'undress' the text and Jane Gallop can see it as a virgin open to penetration. A text may be raped as long as the 'fallacies' of integrity and closure are upheld. Or it may be penetrated in a more friendly way. Gallop can hope to 'engage in some intercourse' with the textual body, to enter without disrespect or violation, believing that 'somewhere there is a desire for dialogue, intercourse, exchange'. (Note here the change from the critic–seducer to a subjectless predication).

I am left uneasy at all this metaphoricity. After all the body does not write and the text does not have a body to clothe and molest. Interpretation is not rape, but a refusal to listen to a text is disrespect.[2]

Along with troping, another favourite method is the question. Derrida had already pioneered criticism through the interrogative, ensuring that, whatever else the question may become, it will not be a mark of insecurity or of any tentativeness. Among the francophile critics, Jardine surely takes the method furthest, presumably espousing Jane Gallop's view that 'This may be a truly feminist gesture to end with questions, not to conclude, but to be open' (p. 32). I will find an example from another piece by Jardine entitled 'Death Sentences: Writing Couples and Ideology' (1986):

> Is there a way to move out of the Family Romance without a certain existential feminism turning men into our mothers?; without revalorizing the phallic mother?; without reinforcing an ideology that requires this particular kind of coupling; or a poetics that must ultimately silence the mother's tongue? Is there a way to write without embalming the past?; without writing tombs? Without dismembering the female body; without killing other women in the name of epistemological purity; without killing our mothers, the mother in us? (p. 95).

Yes, I think there is.

The elusive text

We are not at an impasse in feminist socio-historical analysis, but, under the impact of 'French' criticism, we do seem to be pausing for breath. The tools for the enterprise of rewriting the story of culture and of influencing its future development were forged in the 1970s and they have been sharpened on the theory that has dominated the criticism of the 1980s, necessarily and usefully calling attention to the construction of the present as well as of the past. But, although I see a purpose in encountering Irigaray, Cixous and Kristeva (among others), and in listening to the criticism of Moi, Jacobus and Jardine, I do not see the need to follow them into the supplanting of women by woman or women's voices by ungendered writing in the feminine by men and women. Women are, after all, in history as material entities; they are more than mothers, and they form a kind of non-identical paradigm of the historical process itself. Although the psychoanalytical and deconstructionist theories seem immediately attractive in their decentering of the subject, to decenter it out of existence is to leave ourselves open to remaining locked in the categories that we bring to bear on literature at the specific moment in intellectual history and to mystify history into the timeless model of psychoanalysis. To accept the feminist revisions of Lacanian psychoanalysis entirely is to look at the signifier entirely, and to travel immediately beyond the signified to some sort of formalist metaphysical entity not amenable to alteration or change, although it itself might exist to change a previous metaphysics. Complexities become one great complexity: 'In "woman", I see something . . . above and beyond nomenclatures and ideologies'.

The psychoanalytical approach emphasizing language opens up much. With Freud's help we have seen the difficulty of the relationship of identity to sex, with Lacan's the difficulty of relationship when no fixed essences exist. Such insights must unsettle criticism. But, to me, the psychoanalytical method forecloses on the final elusiveness of a text, which is precisely the presence of history. Literary works give images of women that are not absolutely identical, and the differences among them must be significant. Historical flux and change should not be prematurely ended in symbolic stasis so that women can suffer once and for all an identity fixation on the level of style, releasing action only to the 'woman' of the semiotic. Ultimately the psychoanalytical woman is another reification and the reading taken to preserve her is an erasing of the history of women which we have only just begun to glimpse.

5

Directions

A fascinating feature of the quarrel between French theoretical and American socio-historical feminist criticism in the USA was the use by both sides of the same terms of abuse. Each labelled the other unsubtle, essentialist and conservative. But the adjectives suggested very different notions according to what they qualified; the psychoanalytical critics were labelled conservative because they were anti-reformist in a political sense, while the socio-historical writers achieved the term in an intellectual sense because they still believed in referentiality and the truth of experience.[1] One of the few sophisticated terms which entered both sorts of writing, while retaining some residue of common significance, was ideology. This was a Marxist concept recently made more complex and intellectually appealing by Althusser and Macherey and already long in use by British feminists.

Ideology

The Marxist concept of ideology has been defined, following Althusser, as 'that system of beliefs and assumptions – unconscious, unexamined, invisible – which represent "the imaginary relationship of individuals to their real conditions of existence"'.[2] It is not so much a clearly *false* representation of some truth as the truth itself as we know it, for we are all in ideology, and the various representative systems, such as the political, the religious or the mythical, are reflections of actual relations in which people live. Indeed we experience those relations only in this fictitious order. So ideology is a material reality, a largely unreflected condition of acting and existing within a commonplace world, rather than a group of conscious, voluntary ideas. Individual historical subjects do not choose their ideology or initiate ideology, for we are simply in it before we can in any way become conscious of it. In other words ideology does not set itself up as ideology at all, but instead appears as something unquestionable, as rationality or nature, for example.

For literary analysis, the concept of ideology is especially useful since literature and culture are sites at which ideology is produced and reproduced. In imaginative works a moving ideology can be fixed and brought to consciousness and its contradictions can be made visible. So a concept of ideology can help to explain apparent inconsistencies in past works. For example, in *The German Ideology* Marx saw ideology as aiming to cover up contradictions in the status quo by integrating them into a history or narrative of origins; within ideology there can be an appealing idealization of an earlier outmoded system of values, which may, however, be used to support a later one that it has superseded and to which it may be opposed. Literary analysis can work to uncover this process.

Criticism using the notion of ideology focuses both on what is stressed as intentional and on what appears subliminal, discordant and unintentional. With the notion, we can read against the grain, not aiming to uncover a truth but investigating how a transcendental concept of truth was formed at all. Literature inevitably colludes with ideology, which is in turn inscribed in literary forms, style, conventions, genres and the institution of literary production. But it does not simply affirm, and it can expose and criticize as well as repeat.

There are, I think, dangers when the ideas of ideology are welded to psychoanalysis – which obviously influenced them in their modern formulations – since they may use the message of the absences and silences to obscure the message of what is present, may in other words privilege the presumed deep structure at the expense of the historical surface. But, if we are alive to such dangers, the notion of ideology remains an invaluable tool for feminist analysis.

British feminist criticism

Socialist feminism existed in the USA before the 1980s but it was never a major context of feminist criticism. In Britain, however, it is difficult to speak of feminist criticism in isolation from socialism. British feminism has always had an un-American link with Marxism and politics of the Left; it made a commitment to the collective effort and insisted on the participation of feminist criticism in the wider critique of society.

My main subject so far has been the semi-popular feminist criticism with an historical leaning that has emanated from the USA, a criticism which, I have argued, had strengths and weaknesses precisely because it formed part of a wider, probably class-bound movement. This reformist movement had limited social and academic aims and it achieved a relative but striking success. In Britain the alliance with Marxism worked to prevent feminist criticism from appealing to the unradicalized feminists in the way the books of, say, Showalter and Gilbert and Gubar had done in the States.

It could of course be argued both ways: the small following of feminism and feminist criticism in Britain was due to its impracticality and extremism or it resulted from its refusal to be co-opted as a bourgeois movement. Whatever the case, it has, as a result, not really been pressured into a place in universities and it has hardly been involved in the reassessment of the discipline of literary criticism.

But the strength of the small British enterprise needs stressing. It began with a theoretical sophistication through its interaction with Marxism that gave it a considerable rhetorical advantage. Consequently there has been less of the uninvestigated, unaware, even sloppy criticism that has marked many feminist journals in America. Even in the 1960s and 1970s British feminist criticism was influenced by French deconstruction and psychoanalysis that called into question literary constructs like the subject or the idea of the humanist self, constructs which American feminist criticism found entirely unproblematic. The most impressive examples of such early Marxist feminist criticism much tinged by French theory probably occurred outside university English departments in articles on cinema, such as those printed in *Screen*, and in the interdisciplinary collective work of the Marxist Feminist Literary Collective and the Birmingham Centre for Cultural Studies.

A couple of examples of the approach and subject-matter can be found in the work of Cora Kaplan and Michelle Barrett. Kaplan's article is entitled 'Pandora's box: subjectivity, class and sexuality in socialist feminist criticism'; it occurs in *Making A Difference: Feminist Literary Criticism* (1985) and is reprinted in her own collection *Sea*

Changes. Barrett's article 'Ideology and the cultural production of gender' dates from 1980, but was reprinted in Judith Newton and Deborah Rosenfelt's *Feminist Criticism and Social Change* (1985). Through reprinting it has gained a footnote in which the author contextualizes the piece and points out how it would have been written in 1986.

Cora Kaplan shows how close a criticism informed by a sophisti-cated notion of ideology can approach to psychoanalytical criticism. For example she echoes Jacobus and Moi in her opposition to 'feminist criticism' – by which I presume she means the early American socio-historical variety: 'the most visible, well-defined and extensive tendency within feminist criticism has undoubtedly bought into the white, middle-class, heterosexist values of traditional literary criticism, and threatens to settle down on her own in its cultural suburbs' (p. 147). In addition, Kaplan is as critical of humanism as Jacobus, Moi and Jardine, seeing it as enslaved to the idea that literature is and should be mimetic or realistic representation: 'The humanist critic identifies with the author's claim that the text represents reality, and acts as a sympathetic reader who will test the authenticity of the claim through the evidence of the text.' In opposition she gives us the Marxist critic, who assumes that author and text speak from a position within ideology and that 'claims about fictional truth and authenticity are, in themselves, to be understood in relation to a particular historical view of culture and art which evolved in the Romantic period.' She also gives us the psychoanalytic critic who rejects the possibility of authentic mimetic art at all. This last critic sees the literary text 'as a system of signs that constructs meaning rather than reflecting it, inscribing simultaneously the subjectivity of speaker and reader'. Kaplan insists that we understand the class-bound nature of bourgeois femininity and that we take notice of how writing from within its assumptions constructs us as readers in relation to its particular subjectivity: 'These fictional characters are there as figures in a dream, as constituent structures of the narrative of the dreamer, not as correct reflections of the socially real.'

Although I would not want to follow her psychoanalytic critic into seeing art as entirely non-mimetic, I find Kaplan's aim to bring psychic and social together an attractive project. Her constant stress on ideology and class is a useful corrective to a tendency of American feminist criticism to ignore both. At the same time I regard her criticism of the American socio-historical enterprise as too sweeping.

Possibly it has settled down in some places in the USA, where it can provide careers; it may even have a place in the University of Sussex where Kaplan works. But it has made little headway elsewhere in Britain, neither in the metropolitan centres nor in the provinces and suburbs to continue the image. In addition, the literary criticism with which it seems associated may indeed be in part the old traditional one, but it cannot be entirely so, since gender was not its issue; accepting that a dominant method may have many powers on which to call, I cannot imagine that feminist criticism can be or has been so completely neutralized anywhere.

Michelle Barrett is fearful of uncoupling ideology from the socially real. She affirms her belief in ideology as an important site of the construction of gender but only as part of a social totality rather than as an autonomous practice or discourse. She opposes the emphasis solely on representation in some Marxist and feminist discussions of ideology – in her footnote she extends this to Foucault's work – all of which seem to reject the classical theory of representation as a reflection of specific historical conditions. Representation, she asserts in opposition to Kaplan, is linked to historically constituted real relations and she rejects any criticism that makes the text itself the only basis for analysis. Agreeing with Terry Eagleton, she opposes the notion that criticism, feminist or otherwise, can transcend its conditions of production. It is a salutary deflation of the common hope of a quick marriage – rather than some loose friendship – between materialist feminism and French-inspired formalist and psychoanalytical theory.

In Britain the feminist critical effort in the past and present is not on the whole taking place in the universities but is occurring instead among independent writers, journalists and writing groups and among teachers and students in the polytechnics. Feminist publishing has flourished despite the relative lack of interest in feminist criticism and despite the indifference of the academic establishment. The actual reading of women by a general readership of women, promoted by Virago, Women's Press and Pandora, is far more widespread and various than in the USA. This situation suggests that a certain consciousness by women of women has been spreading in Britain and that, although it has many distinctions from the development in the USA, it also has some parallels – probably these readers are on the whole as middle class as the feminists in the USA. The warning should, however, be given not to confuse the eagerness of publishers, writers and readers for women's books with an influence of feminism on a cultural establishment which in fact remains largely untouched.

Because of its external, 'marginal' position, British feminist criticism could avoid becoming academic like the American variety, separating the literary project from other areas of feminism. So, while American feminist criticism is moving more and more towards the elitist mode, hardening itself with French theory and philosophical or psychoanalytical discourse, many British feminists have continued writing in the creative subjective way that was common to early American feminists. Maggie Humm has recently found a heroine in Adrienne Rich and Moira Monteith's new anthology, *Women's Writing*, mainly written by people outside the universities, avoids academic markings and is subtitled 'A Challenge to Theory' – although its articles cannot, it seems, do without those modish words that have fallen from theory: site and discourse.

Both sides of the Atlantic could benefit from influence by the other. American feminism could do with a political injection and a reminder of the factor of class – stressed by Lillian S. Robinson since the beginning; it could also take a little denting in the inevitable complacency that has followed its relative academic success, some experiencing of the blows that are still rained down on British feminist critics. Meanwhile, the British reading public, which, unlike its equivalent in the USA, has little access to universities, is probably ready for a practical and historical feminist criticism in the American mode, but one which remained more aware of the social moment. Surviving the disenchanted exodus of many of its most vocal exponents to the USA where they can at least be comforted by some institutional success, British feminist criticism might shed some of its self-righteousness and spread itself about, without losing its ideological commitment.

Assimilation

The notion of ideology and the concept of class inform many recent American anthologies that have tried to supplement or escape the formalist and psychoanalytical influence. Given their perspective, they predictably contain some fairly elderly essays by women working in Britain such as Barrett and Kaplan. In *Feminist Criticism and Social Change* Newton and Rosenfelt aim to bring the Marxist perspective to

American feminists shorn of its politically socialist implications – essentially alien to the USA – and labelled materialist feminism. They insist, following the British stance, that gender interacts with other social categories of class and race, that all criticism is ideological, and that aesthetic judgements must be historically relative.

Newton and Rosenfelt strenuously oppose French theory: 'We have committed ourselves to resist a view of literature – formalism – that sees literature and literary critics as divorced from history, a view still perpetrated – despite their air of currency and French fashionableness – by much of the post-structuralist criticism now dominant in Britain and the United States' (p. xvi). Texts should be taken as gestures towards history with political effect and there is no need to overprivilege psychology as the locus of struggle. The editors are as sharp with the liberal humanist pluralism of much American criticism as they are with psychoanalytical theory. Men and women are, they reiterate, ideologically inscribed and not even privileged male authors can be considered free agents. Representation is devious and complex and representative ideologies of gender, caught in texts, must be dismantled if social institutions are to change. Reading of texts thus becomes crucial. Yet, the editors warn, there is no objective reading to be discovered, only a shaping of the cultural use to which writing is always put.

The introduction from Newton and Rosenfelt must serve to place pieces from different times and different cultures. The result is something of a *mélange*, now synthesizing, now simply juxtaposing statements from distinct, unassimilable discourses. The stern anti-formalism of the opening accords oddly with the assertion that 'the discourse suppressed tells us as much as the discourse expressed, for omission throws the margins of a text's production into relief, allowing us to see the limits and the boundaries of what it posits as the real' (p. xxiii). It is difficult to locate omissions without a notion of form.

Occasionally too, despite an emphasis on history, their tendency appears anti-historical, at least in specifics. Although Barrett provides her contextualizing footnote to her article, there is on the whole little upfronting of the historical enterprise of criticism. As in Showalter's *The New Feminist Criticism* and in many other anthologies, composition dates of the essays are hidden away in footnotes or even in closely printed acknowledgements in the front.[3]

The problem of obscuring the history embedded in the collection is avoided in another recent anthology, *Making a Difference: Feminist Literary*

Criticism (1985), edited by Gayle Greene and Coppélia Kahn, which uses only new material. None the less it manages to have the flavour of a diachronic anthology because many of its critics are known for particular views which are reiterated here. More strikingly, the essays have various styles which are reminiscent of the different phases and types of feminist criticism. For example, Sydney Janet Kaplan, historicizing this criticism itself, writes in the personal mode so marked in the early stages of American feminist criticism, while Judith Kegan Gardiner's appealing piece has a curiously old-fashioned quality that makes it seem untouched by the French theoretical concerns discussed by Nelly Furman. The overall impression of the collection is, therefore, fragmentary; different writers follow different systems and different authorities like Saussure, Lacan or Kristeva, and the editors' valiant attempt to synthesize serves only to highlight the plurality. Yet, accepting this plurality, and accepting the book's aim to place feminist criticism more within an interdisciplinary enquiry than in an historical and literary critical context, I found this a remarkable statement and critique of the present condition of our communal effort.

Perhaps it is only after being immersed in the psychoanalytical and post-structuralist subtleties of Mary Jacobus and Alice Jardine that the following seems both slightly simplistic and refreshing:

> the inequality of the sexes is neither a biological given nor a divine mandate, but a cultural construct and therefore a proper subject of study for any humanistic discipline . . . Feminist scholarship . . . restores a female perspective by extending knowledge about women's experience and contributions to culture . . . That men have penises and women do not, that women bear children and men do not, are biological facts which have no determinate meaning in themselves but are invested with various symbolic meanings by different cultures. Feminists do, however, find themselves confronting one universal – that, whatever power or status may be accorded to women in a given culture, they are still, in comparison to men, devalued as "the second sex". Feminist scholars study *diverse* social constructions of femaleness and maleness in order to understand the *universal* phenomenon of male dominance (pp. 1–2).

Greene and Kahn emphasize that 'the oppression of woman is both material reality, originating in material conditions, and a psychological phenomenon, a function of the way women and men perceive one another and themselves.' This seems a useful emphasis, but I think they have a tendency to go too far towards seeing these material conditions and psychological phenomena from other disciplines such as anthropology and psychoanalysis, those disciplines that appear to offer rigour and control to flabby literary criticism.[4] In addition I find them leaning too far in their bias towards the clearly oppressed. In some of the essays, class is subtly considered, but, in the introduction, it results in some unhelpful antipathies, such as a dislike of a history of exceptional women. Until recently women who wrote were small in number relative to the population as a whole; inevitably they were mainly from the upper and middle classes since these were more or less the only ones who had access to pens and publishing, and, by definition, they were exceptional. It would be wonderful to have more writing of working-class women, but, until it is discovered in the seventeenth and eighteenth centuries, for example, I would not want to downgrade what is there or exclude it from serious attention on the basis of its class origin – although it remains essential that this origin be mentioned.

I have one slightly carping criticism of the political and interdisciplinary enterprise of Greene and Kahn – as indeed of Newton and Rosenfelt. Like French theoretical criticism, it rarely seems to result in any sustained involvement with texts though it may include stimulating and provocative suggestions; language and literariness are frequently downplayed and Newton and Rosenfelt separate themselves from critics with a 'more cultural or traditionally literary orientation'. In addition, certain exemplary stories, usually short, are constantly treated, for example Freud's case history of Dora in French-inspired criticism or Isak Dineson's 'The Blank Page' and Charlotte Perkins Gilman's 'The Yellow Wallpaper' in more historical versions.

The widening of literature

Some danger to our enterprise derives from the very success of the early stages of tool-forging. Without much further thinking about what we are doing, it would be quite easy now simply to use the various sets of tools at our disposal on canonized women, either those in the male tradition or those now emerging in the female Norton version. So there would be, for example, feminist readings, following Gilbert and Gubar, of the Brontës, Woolf, Eliot, Austen and Barrett Browning in one series and Lacanian or Kristevan readings of the same women in another. In such a project we would be amply supported by a publishing industry willing and eager for feminist books in handy and marketable series, but far less eager to promote individual books that propose the abolition of that canon which makes the job of publishing so manageable. But feminist literary history should not burn itself out as an alternative approach, however acceptable to the establishment, and become yet another rereading of the canon.

Much is probably going to come from groups of women who identify themselves as feminist and something else, like black or lesbian, either as critics or creative writers.[5] Much can also come from those who, like the collective writers of the Birmingham Centre, do not see literature in isolation or accept a privileged status for any forms. The study of popular culture and hitherto unacceptable works can help to destabilize the reading of privileged texts, prevent institutionalization, and emphasize critical self-awareness. It may, in addition, persuade us to question any canon that proclaims its naturalness and interrupt any hardening of critical or literary formations.

In the past, writing on popular culture was often separated from writing on elite culture. Critics accepted the assumption of Q. D. Leavis in *Fiction and the Reading Public* (1932), that mass art was bad for the mind and must be opposed. The detrimental effect was theorized during the 1930s by Theodor Adorno and the Frankfurt School as a division between an art that is dominated by ideology and one that resists ideology. Nowadays there seems less clarity about a distinction between mass and elite art; the enormous valuation of modernist expression, which has marked French theoreticians and feminists, as well as the writers of the Frankfurt School, can be seen historically and can be disturbed by the idea of the commodification of any art. Consumer society and its changes of fashion affect mass art and modernist experimentation alike, as Fredric Jameson and others have argued.[6] Distinctions have been broken down and collusion and compromise are found in elite works, and criticism and subversion in the mass. It is no longer possible to ignore popular art, nor to dismiss it as a conspiracy of capitalist producers.[7]

Speculation

Another way forward is always through daring speculation that does not immediately harden into generalization. Alice Jardine provides an example in 'Spaces for Further Research: Male Paranoia' in *Gynesis*, in which she out-Foucault's Foucault in adventurous speculative history. Starting from the idea of epistemological breaks in Western thought proposed by the French thinkers Michel Foucault and Jean-Joseph Goux, she wonders whether, if they exist at all, these breaks may in fact derive from the coming into discourse of women. The medieval concern for women, the *querelle des femmes*, produced both women writers and an upsurge of feminist thought; between 1300 and 1600 'woman' was put into discursive circulation in entirely new ways. The late eighteenth and nineteenth centuries are similarly marked by an obsessive discursivity of women; women again became the subjects as well as the objects of discourse. Jardine asks of the epistemological breaks located in these periods, 'Could it be that the "two major transitions in Western thought" might be directly linked to the subject (of) woman?' (p. 96). This is a wonderful question to ask, raising many other questions – as well as doubts about the activity of postulating such immense historical abstractions at all. We should wait for a consider-able time before firmly answering it.

Another example occurs in Sandra Gilbert and Susan Gubar's article, 'Tradition and the Female Talent' (1984). Looking critically at much-valued modernism, they speculate that it might be seen as a response to the anxieties of male artists about their female contempora-ries. Noting that modernist formulations of societal breakdown consistently employ specifically sexual imagery – especially that of male impotence and female potency – they argue that a misogynistic reaction against the rise of literary women may well have been a motive for, as well as a theme in, modernism and its desire both for elitist linguistic innovation and for a tradition of male precursors.

Feminist literary history

The patriarchal nature of language and culture must inform the tellings of history. This is the genre from which women have been especially excluded and into which they are now entering as objects of study and as writing subjects. Yet there has been in recent years an assault on any notion that a discourse termed historical – or fictional – could denote reality; the result is a problematizing both of history and of the connection of literature and history. In place of history, we are getting histories, different and infinitely numerous itineraries through the past. So, where the eighteenth- and nineteenth-century novelists seemed to absorb the project of history into fiction, our own age is obsessed with history as a series of fictions. Women are, then, entering history just as the distinction between the historical account and the happening or the something out there is most unstable, when it is becoming clear that that happening has no natural configuration, no necessary articulation at all. These developments certainly allow women into the construction of history – they may in fact be connected with their arrival just as the destabilizing of the Renaissance or of modernism may be associated with women's appearance, as Jardine and Gilbert and Gubar have speculated – but they may also allow another kind of marginalization through the idea of the deconstruction of *all* history before a 'women's history' has been described.

So what histories can we use? Not I think the progressive one, neither Whig history nor Chateaubriand's fatalist history, the almost providential retelling of the past to capture a predetermined progress. Some early feminist critical history sounded a little like this, with women writers, especially those labelled as feminist, moving nearer and nearer through time towards a truth we alone had fully grasped. Instead, we should aim for some reconstructions of the past that allow its richness, texture, and strangeness to emerge.

In her introduction to *Tulsa Studies in Women's Literature*, Fall 1986, Shari Benstock celebrates the institution of Gilbert and Gubar's *Norton Anthology*. But in considering the structure of the volume – history, women's history, women's writing – she warns against two assumption: first that of women encased in the more important traditional history, which inevitably turns out to be 'a history of *men*'s accomplishments, of *men*'s concerns (politics, religion, economics, etc.), a record of the development of patriarchy', and, second, that of women existing in a separate female history: 'Women writers (like women) do not have a separate history, do not live lives outside their temporal and spatial circumstamnces, do not escape cultural, social, and political imperatives'. I believe both her points are true ones, but the opposition she makes here – based of course on the polarization in the *Norton Anthology* – between man's history and a woman's history, even the non-separatist one she proposes, may be limiting. Many studies assume a separation of male public and civic history and female private herstory, with the result that the 'politics, religion and economics' which form male history quickly become men's domain alone and we are in danger of forgetting that history is not gendered, only the telling. What comes forward as women's history, such as changes in fashion of breast feeding, marriage settlements, contraception and the treatment of widows, is profoundly relevant to women's writing, but so are civic events, economic changes and religious and political controversy in which many women played a part and which affected the organization of their lives. Balance is needed. Menstruation is not the *whole* of the female experience.

Nina Baym has warned against the laudable interest in women's private writing; in our enthusiasm for diaries and letters we are in danger of forgetting that women from an early period wrote directly in interventionist modes and wanted to succeed as professional authors. We may be forgetting that women took part in religious struggles, wrote political pamphlets, and in many periods were connected with the government. To some extent it has been the stress on the Victorian domestic woman writer, so much a feature of American feminist criticism of the 1970s, that has pushed the typical woman into retirement and passivity. Even Ruth Perry in her admirable biography of Mary Astell (1986), which fully presents a writing woman engaged with the intellectual and political controversies of her time, can mention in passing that to write for money appeared ill-bred for women until the mid-nineteenth century. It is hard to imagine Fanny Burney and even Jane Austen, both much concerned with the pounds and pence of their enterprise, fitting into this generalization.

Feminist literary criticism should, then, range widely for its history and questions, using and abusing men when necessary, always aware of the partial nature of the historical record and taking as much as possible into account. So we cannot simply ignore the traditional constructed literary history, for example, but we can historicize and so destabilize it, just as we can, dimly, start to historicize our own patterns of thought and open up ourselves to criticism from the past. Such openness can occur if we can avoid too quickly establishing limiting continuities and identities between past and present that bully the past and its literature out of their specificity and materiality.

The potential of the historical feminist approach has not yet been fulfilled, an approach that disrupts the canon and all readings and is informed by an apprehension of ideology as material and psychological, but which eschews the tendency towards the single history of psychoanalysis and is wary of the quick assertion that all histories are but rhetoric. It recognizes that empiricism is indeed already theorized but that empirical study still allows challenges on its edges, where theory alone may codify and reify the prejudice of the moment. The historical approach provides tools like any other, but it cannot, in the manner of some of the approaches I have been criticizing, fit texts like a grid. History opens up the possibility of strangeness, while the notion of ideology interposes, in Marilyn L. Williamson's words 'the sexual ideologies of the past between the critic and the text, and in doing so balances the inevitable biases the critic brings to the interpretive process'.[8] What it requires is close literary work which will pry open a history that has been closed to us and which will again be closed to us – albeit with more attractive closure – if we prematurely psychoanalyse, destabilize, or historically generalize on too slim and haphazard a base.

If feminist literary history or historical criticism can keep its integrity, it can gain much from associating outside, and I agree with Alice Jardine, that 'If feminism is to remain radical and not become but patchwork for a patriarchal fabric ripped apart by the twentieth century' it must consider 'what kinds of alliances' it will be able to form 'with the most radical modes of thought produced by that century' (*Gynesis*, p. 64). Mary Jacobus extends this useful point. She notes that American historical criticism, with its somewhat naïve devotion to pluralism risks turning feminism into yet another ingredient in an existing plurality of literary criticism. Instead, it should constitute a critique of that pluralized *mélange*.

One form of such a critique could result from the increased critical awareness of historical specificity, as well as a recognition that the separation of surface and implied messages according to our present requirements – our common method of assaulting the past – may represent desire in us rather than in the author. At the very least works of the past should be able to inform us as readers of the differences between present and past perceptions, however flawed our apprehension of them. At the same time we need to learn from the Jacobus kind of approach that language does tell a great deal more than we have been accustomed to hearing. If we stay entirely at the level of theory or unexamined history we may never find 'herstory' at all but remain locked into logical critical extremes, the fallacies committed by both strict empiricists and psychoanalytical theorists.

Feminist literary history can also learn something from the ideas of what has been termed new historicist criticism. This has been much celebrated and abused and is indeed so various that it deserves almost all epithets. But in its more successful manifestations, it does offer a method of specific historical study that takes into account the workings of ideology and the way that the artistic text reproduces that inviting ideology. Criticism can help to caution the reader against this invitation; at the same time, as Jerome J. McGann, a celebrant of the new historicist approach, has argued, work cannot and should not be reduced to pure ideological statement, undifferentiated from any other work, for such a reduction becomes transhistorical:

> all inherited works of literature have it in their power to force a critical engagement with any present form of thought (whether a critical or an ideological form) by virtue of the historical differentials which separate every present from all the past – by virtue of those differentials which draw the present and the past together across the field of concrete and particular differences (*The Romantic Ideology*, p. 14).

Genre

Another fruitful, I think vitally necessary, development is the study of genre. Not in the old-fashioned way of classification and prescription but as a system of historical and literary expectations and assumptions. The critic emphasizing genre cannot use history simply as a kind of background, as a given from another discipline which will illuminate our own. She is forced to probe ideology in its specific deployment in literary form. Such a method works to deconstruct the powerful ideology of established literary periods or movements, like the Augustan, the Romantic, or the Modern, in such a way that the critic can begin to avoid being dominated by the self-representations of their exponents. The method can also be added to the study of popular culture so that genres that have been despised as popular or feminine can be illuminated and the uncanonized can be connected with the canonized in startling ways, to break down the 'aristocracy of discourse'.

Genre concerns communication; it is, as Alastair Fowler has argued in *Kinds of Literature* (1982), an instrument of meaning, a sort of hermeneutic instruction, the basis of conventions that make literary communication possible. These are mutable through time and so amenable to historical investigation; indeed they require it, for otherwise they can function in static prescriptive ways. To ignore genre is often to be led astray by a momentary critical fashion and to be pulled away from any consideration of intention in the most obvious sense, what literary gestures originally signalled or what strangeness the author conveyed in her disrupting of expectation. Did Mary Wollstonecraft startlingly interrupt her texts with her personal emotions or are such interruptions common in the genres she followed? Is the repetition in *A Vindication of the Rights of Woman* an indication of unrepressed feeling and haste or an example of the rhetorical habit of polemical writers practised at least since Quintilian – or, of course, both?

A good illustration of such genre study is Tania Modleski's *Loving with a Vengeance* (1982), a beginning rather than an exhaustive study of certain mass art genres like the Gothic and the Harlequin romance. The study makes use of some psychoanalytical assumptions but it situates them in the works and in the responses that the works seem to demand, with the result that it discovers changing patterns rather than a single pattern of stimulation and resolve or a unitary aim of social conservatism, so often assumed for romance. By remaining at the level of genre, Modleski avoids some of the simplifications of early historical feminist criticism which found constant patterns of subversion wherever it looked.

I will give a specific example of the use of genre for Jane Austen. In the beginning of the feminist critical enterprise there was considerable effort to bring Jane Austen into the useable female past, to rescue her from her high reputation as mother of the great tradition of F. R. Leavis and highest point of the rising novel of Ian Watt, in short to bring her into the sisterhood. Gilbert and Gubar make an appropriation in *The Madwoman in the Attic* by cutting her loose from tradition, genre and class and making her a gendered being first and foremost, an exponent of their subversive thesis of women's writing. So her work grows duplicitous and secretive, forming texts that demand deconstruction rather than an appreciation of surface meaning, texts that acknowledge the furtive and aware female reader not the male appropriator. Gilbert and Gubar find Austen repeatedly satirizing fathers who represent the patriarchy against which she is pressing – as these fathers fail, so does the patriarchal system – and investigating female ties through which women manipulate and manoeuvre.

Although an exciting recuperation of Austen at the moment when it was made, in the late 1970s, there remain problems with this kind of reading, not least because it privileges as context and base the male literary tradition which Austen is seen to be subverting. At the same time it largely ignores the female context, the many women writers whom we rarely read now in whose works there are similar treatments of fathers, only a great deal more condemnatory, and similar deployments of female relationships, only a great deal more euphoric and political.

The unworthy humbled patriarch is one of the stock characters of sentimental female fiction of the mid- and late eighteenth century; he occurs in Jane Austen, however, only when he has no wife to be even further condemned. In her treatment of female ties outside the family, Austen is largely hostile, from Isabella and Catherine in *Northanger Abbey* to Harriet and Emma in *Emma*, whose friendship must subside on marriage, while the more sophisticated, eccentric or wiser older woman, so much a feature of the novels of Fanny Burney, Charlotte Smith and Maria Edgeworth, rarely fascinates the young Austen heroine and never provides an adequate guide to life.

Indeed, from the point of view of the female genre of her time, which by the late eighteenth century already formed a powerful ideology in itself, it is worth considering what Austen manifestly leaves out and what such writers as Mary Wollstonecraft and Maria Edgeworth put in; one example is the frequent feminization of the hero who, in the popular sentimental female novel and in its gothic extensions such as Radcliffe's *The Mysteries of Udolpho*, often lacks the economic power given to the heroine on the final pages and who avoids displaying the overtopping behaviour so common in the villains. In the dashing or economically potent figures of Mr Tilney, Mr Darcy, Mr Knightley and Captain Wentworth, Austen clearly breaks with this element of female fiction.

If, then, we read Jane Austen in connection with contemporary women novelists, we see her treating and varying standard motifs of the female genre of heterosexual love and marriage; she is concerned to display less a social panorama than the inner life of a single woman and to avoid generalizing to the patriarchal system her indictment of individual failings. In these habits, she is writing in conversation with, rather than indifference to, her sister authors whom she herself constantly read.

A beginning of a much more generically aware literary-historical study of Austen has been made in Marilyn Butler's *Jane Austen and the War of Ideas*. This was somewhat mistimed when it appeared in 1975, since, although it put forward a very persuasive reading, it did so without much awareness of developing feminist critical thought. None the less, dated as it is, it is still the most useful corrective to the more heroic and more initially exciting but essentially ahistorical and ungeneric approach of Gilbert and Gubar; it presents the author as part of a literary environment and as articulating common ideological assumptions. Oxford University Press has decided to reissue Butler's book with a new preface which places the original enterprise within the project of feminist criticism.

In this preface Butler takes to task early American feminist criticism of Austen which read her outside of her time, arguing that it is possible to see her as subversive only when we look at her in isolation or in some diachronic perspective that generalizes about women's secrecy and lack of involvement with political and sociological questions:

> this decontextualising is a manoeuvre that permits the critic a licence itself anything but critical, in the most useful sense of self-critical. It allows the original writer to evade meaningful challenges from her contemporaries, and to take the colluding critic with her into an unsocial, unspecific, timeless zone called art. Art, an area set up by post-romantic intellectuals as a tax-haven where there is nothing to pay.

To deny that the author lives in any way in the work is also a gesture in time, conditioned by our own historical moment of criticism in high reaction to the over presence of the author in Romantic art. To deny Austen her male and female context is to avoid noticing the feminized genre of the novel in which she was working, as well as the various 'discourses of political theory and of behaviour, religion and morals' to which she refers. It is to take comfort with Gilbert and Gubar in the representation of the past as an 'unmitigated scandal'.

6
Readings of Mary Wollstonecraft

Wollstonecraft has experienced criticism, including feminist criticism, in a rather different way from her more establishment sister, Jane Austen. Partly because she left so full a record of her version of her life, she has been open to appropriation by various psychological methods. In the 1947, for example, she was subjected to the vicious attentions of Ferdinand Lundberg and Marynia Farnham in *Modern Woman: The Lost Sex*. Writing at the moment when women were being translated from war workers into domestic and sexy objects, bolstered by the 'feminine mystique', the authors created out of Wollstonecraft's life a cautionary tale of penis envy and gender confusion, inevitably punctuated by suicide attempts; in this view it seems to have been both ironic and retributive that she died in the supremely feminine way of childbirth.

For the early feminist 'herstorians' Wollstonecraft was easily assimilable as the founding mother, the first feminist, the almost sacred progenitor towards whose sufferings and struggles we as her children should take a stance of reverence. In some places in North America criticizing her was as risky a business as deconstructing Virginia Woolf.

More recently, Wollstonecraft's writings have been the object of far more sophisticated and persuasive psychoanalysis and historical deconstruction, for example by Mary Poovey, in *The Proper Lady and the Woman Writer* (1984). Through attending to her language, in a section subtitled 'Man's Discourse, Woman's Heart', Poovey traces Wollstonecraft's partial development out of the crippling strictures of feminine propriety by way of the vacillating dichotomy of reason and feeling.

In *A Vindication of the Rights of Men*, Poovey argues, Wollstonecraft aspires to 'be a man' through her use of rationalist language which hides her female flaw of feeling beneath the mask of male discourse. In the next work, *A Vindication of the Rights of Woman*, she makes a bourgeois assault on behalf of individual effort against aristocratic privilege and passivity. But this self-indulgence and passivity are most marked in women who have been defined by the culture first and foremost as sexual beings. Wollstonecraft fears sexual desire in women, and in herself, and implies that it might be even more voracious and so more blameworthy than male desire. Maturation is, then, stripped of its sexual character, and the imagination, directing towards spiritual gratification, is separated from a loathsome appetite. In her final novel, *The Wrongs of Woman*, which she wrote after she had experienced passion and sexual love with Gilbert Imlay and William Godwin, Wollstonecraft connects female sexuality with the bourgeois ideology of marriage. But she resists the implications of the very insights her story dramatizes; instead she holds onto the sentimental feminine system that blasts sexuality. She thus falls victim to the sentimental idealism she half criticizes in her chief character, Maria; 'Sexuality is virtually the only human quality that is described in this novel with any degree of physical detail, and the descriptions . . . suggest grotesqueness, violence, and contamination' (p. 110). In addition she castigates the imagination which leads now to romantic disillusion rather than to spirituality as in the earlier *The Rights of Woman*.

Although there is certainly a mingled development and stasis in Wollstonecraft, I have some doubts about this complex reading. The nexus of ideas here – aristocracy, passivity, feminine desire, sexuality, sentimentalism – occurs in her writings. Yet, when one considers the frequent connection in contemporary female fiction of passivity only with *feminine* aristocracy – the male aristocrat is usually supremely active, as the various Sir Clements and Sir Jaspers indicate – it might be as possible to see passivity as a kind of feminine sexual power indeed, but also as an appropriation of the *only* power, albeit modified, that women could see other women as holding within society. The constant fantasy of aristocratic birth in the feminine sentimental novel was much mocked by male critics such as William Beckford, but it answered a very real craving for a significance that could occur without the active effort from which middle-class women were debarred.

I will come back to the problem of the imagination and sexuality which Poovey raises. But first it might be useful to show to those unfamiliar with Wollstonecraft's writings how ambiguous, equivocal and just plain muddled she can be – at the level of plot, language, chapter and paragraph – how open therefore to varying interpretations.

In *The Wrongs of Woman* she is criticizing in pretty conventional ways the boy's upbringing in self-indulgence (Richardson had put similar views into the mouths of both Pamela and Mr.B himself): 'Accustomed to submit to every impulse of passion, and never taught, like women, to restrain the most natural, and acquire instead of the bewitching frankness of nature, a factitious propriety of behaviour, every desire became a torment that bore down all opposition' (p. 42). Here the paragraph on men suddenly becomes a vehicle for bitterness on behalf of women.

Mary Jacobus takes up the problem of autobiographical intrusion in her treatment of Wollstonecraft in 'The Difference of View' (1979). Like Poovey, she sees her trying to gain access to male-dominated culture through her appropriation in *A Vindication of the Rights of Woman* of the language of enlightenment reason. Yet for women this inevitably becomes alienating, repressive of female desire. In Wollstonecraft's later works, the marginalized language of feeling connected with hysteria and madness returns and necessarily allies the self with insanity. Displaced onto writing, this produces a movement of imaginative and linguistics excess, swamping for the moment any distinction of author and character. So Wollstonecraft writes of madness in *The Wrongs of Woman*:

> What is the view of the fallen column, the mouldering arch, of the most exquisite workmanship, when compared with this living memento of the fragility, the instability, of reason, and the wild luxuriancy of noxious passions? Enthusiasm turned adrift, like some rich stream overflowing its banks, rushes forward with destructiuve velocity, inspiring a sublime concentration of thought. *Thus thought Maria* – These are the ravages over which humanity must ever mournfully ponder . . . . It is not over the decaying productions of the mind, embodied with the happiest art, we grieve most bitterly. The view of what has been done by man, produces a melancholy, yet aggrandizing, sense of what remains to be achieved by human intellect; but a mental convulsion, which, like the devastation of an earthquake, throws all the elements of thought and imagination into confusion, makes contemplation giddy, and we fearfully ask on what ground we ourselves stand. [Jacobus's italics]

Mary Jacobus's immediate comment on this passage is, 'This is what it means for women to be on the side of madness as well as silence.'

Rejecting the essentialism that she still finds in most readings of Wollstonecraft, she sees this 'feminist sublime' as a breach in the male text through an explosion of sensibiltiy. Madness is both resolution and articulation of utopian desire, and it gestures past the impasse played out in the author herself. It transgresses literary boundaries as the stucture shakes to show the 'conditions of possibility within which women's writing exists', the moment of desire and rupture (pp. 15–16).

It seems to me that in this reading theory has overwhelmed history and genre. Penetrating the surface of the text, Jacobus has ignored the surface of history, of class and politics, for example, to find critical excess and turn her subject into a kind of shadowy Virginia Woolf. Stimulating though the description of madness is – the picture of Wollstonecraft contemplating insanity, like an early Jane Eyre after Gilbert and Gubar – it should not be isolated from the specific historical context that makes of madness a stance of the period, a trope of sentimental fiction, as well as an individual posture.[1]

In contemporary fiction insanity was often the necessary context for the flourishing of redemptive feminine suffering. The characters in *The Wrongs of Woman* (1798) are imprisoned in an asylum; a decade earlier the heroine of Wollstonecraft's sentimental first novel, *Mary. A Fiction* (1788) had longed for madness as an escape from excessive sensibility, and Maria in *The Wrongs of Woman* concludes that the condition of all women is already a form of madness; all are in a way trapped in a prison-asylum. But the later heroine is criticized precisely for her tendency to fall for sentimental rhetoric and projections and to confuse narrative and metaphor with the material world. After all, then, the madhouse in which she is trapped is not metaphoric but a specific and legal institution.

In addition, when Wollstonecraft was writing, there was further resonance from the spectacle of an insane king, authority gone mad. Her earliest discussion of madness occurs in this context and, whatever her additional personal experience might have been – Emily Sunstein in her biography *A Different Face* speculates about an insane brother – she contemplated madness most lengthily and primarily in a political context, *A Vindication of the Rights of Men*. This work was an answer to Edmund Burke, who had attacked the insane king as divinely afflicted.

Madness is for Wollstonecraft individual misery and a breakdown of regal authority, a personal and political problem. It appears an unnecessary marginalizing of her and her writing to take her out of the history in which she played and intended to play a part, so making the madness she contemplated *identical* with the disorder of any writing woman disrupting her text at any time. Surely this is to confine her to the attic indeed. It is also, I think, to misread. The madness of authority and culture in its degeneration frightens Wollstonecraft, not culture and authority itself as in Jacobus's reading.

So to the point of the intrusive autobiography mentioned by both Poovey and Jacobus. In *The Wrongs of Woman* Wollstonecraft is writing out of a constructed character of the compassionate female, made more forcible by an intrusion of autobiography. This may be a disruption as Poovey and Jacobus read it or a failure of 'art' as Virginia Woolf reads a similar intrusion in Charlotte Brontë's *Jane Eyre*. But it is also a feature of the female novel of sensibility, a feature contained by the genre and therefore expected by readers, who had already noted in previous fiction the autobiographical complaints of Charlotte Smith and the personal pain of Mary Hays.

Jacobus calls this intrusion 'a break of fictional decorum', through which writing enacts protest as well as articulating it. But Wollstone-craft is still partly writing within a genre which is marked by this habit and which is, furthermore, limited in its reception by precisely the critical assumption that a female author would be peculiarly associated with her writing. So it cannot really be described as a breach of fictional decorum. While I would agree that the passage Jacobus quotes does articulate a protest, I do not see it *enacting* it. The genre of women's writing avoids the fiction of authorial control and objectivity, and so such an intrusion as Wollstonecraft makes can be seen as slippage only if one ignores generic considerations.

The final reading of Wollstonecraft I want to look at is contained in Cora Kaplan's 'Pandora's Box' in *Making a Difference*. In this essay Wollstonecraft is taken as representative, the first woman to discuss fully the psychological expression of femininity. She is seen as deeply implicated in the project of feminist humanism and caught in the ideology of independent subjectivity or of the autonomous inner life, which Kaplan sees as precisely founded on the exclusion of gender, class and race. Wollstonecraft opposes an essentialist sexual ideology which would accept the complementarity of genders; instead she sees women's psychic life as substantially identical with men's, but distorted through vicious and systematic patriarchal inscription. Social reforms alone can prevent women from becoming regressively obsessed with sexuality and feeling in the way Rousseau had constructed them in *Emile*. 'It is Mary Wollstonecraft who first offered women this fateful choice between the opposed and moralized bastions of reason and feeling, which continues to determine much feminist thinking', Kaplan states (p. 155). In another article 'Wild Nights: Pleasure/Sexuality/ Feminism' (1983; printed in *Sea Changes*) she further accuses Wollstonecraft of setting up 'heartbreaking conditions for women's liberation – a little death, the death of female pleasure' (p. 39).

Female sensuality or desire becomes for Wollstonecraft a contagion, 'In women the irrational, the sensible, even the imaginative are all drenched in an overpowering and subordinating sexuality'. In *The Wrongs of Woman*, this distaste is less evident but 'only maternal feeling survives as a positively realized element of the passionate side of the psyche.' Kaplan's Wollstonecraft betrays 'the most profound anxiety about the rupturing force of female sexuality' (p. 41).

I would like to modify each of the readings I have been describing by noting that the frequently discovered distaste for sexuality is not so much distaste for the desiring woman (when 'we' watch displays of sex and sentiment in women we are supposed to have an emotion 'similar to what we feel when children are playing or animals sporting') as of women and men as sexual and so selfish beings ('a master or mistress of a family ought not to continue to love each other with passion'). Women are dangerous, it seems to me, mainly as the *objects* of desire: a man should not 'lavish caresses on the overgrown child, his wife'. Sexuality is a depravity of the appetite which weakens the frame and coarsens the spirits certainly, but the worst effect of this coarsening is in men. I question, too, whether it is fair to drench the imagination in sexuality as Kaplan does here. While the paeons to sensibility that mark the early novel *Mary, A Fiction*, have disappeared in *The Rights of Woman*, the imagination is left strangely above it all in a rather surplus position much like God.

Perhaps it is for this reason that fantasy can be saved for some activity in *The Wrongs of Woman*. Poovey and Kaplan in particular see the imagination in that novel as colluding with a limiting sexuality. Yet, although the dream of sexual passion with the hero, Darnford, with whom Maria is locked up in the asylum, inevitably grows sour, the author explicitly states that the dreams and the imaginative moments have value. Undoubtedly female sexuality leads to the victimization of women who are oppressed in the novel whether or not they understand their condition correctly. Yet to exist at all pleasurably in a brutalized world requires an element of fantasy, of make-believe. Sexual love, transitory and falsely constructed though it may be, seems a necessary step to female maturation, a good in itself, providing that it exists for itself and does not become a commercial counter to be used in exchange for money in maintenance or marriage. Asexuality in women, which had been translated into virtue or chastity in *Mary, A Fiction* and into coldness in *A Vindication of the Rights of Woman*, now becomes a failing; in complete opposition to the earlier novel, it also becomes the antagonist of a desirable sensibility:

> When novelists or moralists praise as a virtue, a woman's coldness of constitution, and want of passion; and make her yield to the ardour of her lover out of sheer compassion, or to pomote a frigid plan of future comfort, I am disgusted. They may be good women, in the ordinary acceptation of the phrase, and do no harm; but they appear to me not to have those 'finely fashioned nerves,' which render the senses exquisite. They may possess tenderness; but they want that fire of the imagination, which produces *active* sensibility, and *positive* virtue . . . . Truth is the only basis of virtue; and we cannot, without depraving our minds, endeavour to please a lover or husband, but in proportion as he pleases us. (p. 153)

As Cora Kaplan argues, Wollstonecraft *does* valorize motherhood – although I do not believe that this is the only state she approves. But it seems to me that in *The Wrongs of Woman* she avoids her earlier essentialist assumptions about nurturing women. Women remain more tender than men, as suggested in *Mary. A Fiction*, but it is because they have developed this quality under adversity since they labour 'under a portion of misery, which the constitution of society seems to have entailed on all women'. It is not far from Jane Austen's point in *Persuasion*, that women are more faithful in love than men because they are confined at home where their feelings prey on them.

Kaplan's conclusion that 'By defending women against Rousseau's denial of their reason, Wollstonecraft unwittingly assents to his negative eroticized sketch of their emotional lives' seems unfair in the light of *The Wrongs of Woman*, as does her quick assimilation of Wollstonecraft into the malaise of modern feminism: 'It is interesting and somewhat tragic that Wollstonecraft's paradigm of women's psychic economy still profoundly shapes modern feminist consciousness'. Which comes first, Wollstonecraft or our construction of her? Is Wollstonecraft the isolated psyche she sometimes seems to think she is herself or are we dealing with a multiplicity of literary conventions and notions that gain resonance from reiteration across a host of women writers? Is there a personal failure such as Poovey implies or is it we who have imposed a progressive notion on the achievement of lives? After all, Wollstonecraft died in childbirth, a death that was not retribution, premeditation or surrender.

As with Austen I would like to argue for a greater historicizing of Wollstonecraft and the record of her life. Kaplan insists on intertextuality, hearing Wollstonecraft 'against the polyphonic lyricism of Paine, Godwin and the dozen of ephemeral pamphleteers who were celebrating the fact and prospect of the revolution' ('Wild Nights', p. 38). What of the not so ephemeral female writers? The context of other women and men writers, of the tradition of women thinking about themselves, of self-consciousness expressed in sentimental language, and of political and social involvement enriches Wollstonecraft so that her notion of herself as a lonely signpost bespattered with criticism and misogyny becomes a strangely communal image, as ideological a creation in its own way as the assaulting dirt.

The studies of Wollstonecraft by Poovey, Jacobus and Kaplan are among the most subtle and coherent ones we have. But I think each might be modified by closer attention to the genres of women, to the socio-history in which Wollstonecraft intervened and to the writers who were being read and thought about when she was writing. Attention to them would prevent her isolation and her reduction to a single and yet generalized psyche. Wollstonecraft is not the only maker of her own terms. And although, as Kaplan argues, she sets up the parameters of a debate that is still in progress, it is as necessary to see distinctions between her intervention in that debate and our own as it is to find continuities.

Wollstonecraft and history

There is little sense of history in *The Rights of Woman* and classes are fixed; the idea of the rights of man is not seen as the product of an historical moment and of a gendered society but as the expression of reason accepted as the universal transcendental panacea. In her views Wollstonecraft is undoubtedly caught in the contradictions of the enlightenment, the 'dialectic of enlightenment' to use the phrase of

Horkheimer and Adorno, in which rationality ultimately produces its opposite since it take to itself the exchange principle in which everything is reduced to the abstract equivalence of everything else, in the service of a universal exchange.[2] In *The Rights of Woman* Wollstonecraft links the notion of rights to the commercial values of the self-made man, flourishing self-reliantly without aristocratic privilege; then she simply extends it to women. But, in *The Wrongs of Woman*, the enlightenment-inspired belief that rights are unproblematical and individual and that women have the same ones as men, as well as the hope that men will grant these rights as women prove their worthiness, is replaced by a more pessimistic acceptance that the very idea of rights for women is utopian. The assumption of women's protest into a general unproblematic one was, it seems, premature.

A route forward was history itself, the writing of it in fiction. For an understanding of this it is necessary to remember another generic context beyond the romantic novel, Romantic poetry.

There are women poets in the late eighteenth and early nineteenth century but there are no women Romantic poets, giving that phrase all the privileged force it has acquired within later literary studies. No one, however, denied that there were prose writers of distinction.[3] Indeed, more than at any other period before or since, the manifestly distinguished novelists were female. On the whole, then, men were celebrating the timeless epiphanic moment in such works as *The Prelude, Jerusalem, The Fall of Hyperion* and *Prometheus Unbound*, while women novelists, Austen's 'injured body', were making their mark through such prosaic works as *The Wrongs of Woman, Frankenstein, The Mysteries of Udolpho, Self-Control, The Wanderer, Belinda, Sense and Sensibility* and *Mansfield Park*. Male critics have explained the absence (if not the presence) in various ways: Yvor Winters considered women were simply unable to manipulate the codes of high art and so had insufficient wit to write Romantic poetry. Other believed that, in F. R. Leavis's phrase, women were simply not 'at the fine point of consciousness' of their time.

These, together with most other critics, automatically privilege poetry. (In similar fashion Cixous praises poetry at the expense of the novel, seeing the latter as an ally of representation and the former as the ally of the unconscious.) More precisely, they privilege *Romantic* poetry. That is, they extract from the work of those male writers labelled Romantic an aesthetic transcendental component to the exclusion of other more political, less idealistic ones. What I too am isolating in these poets is, then, true of a tendency in most of their careers – that is, a movement towards greater subjectivity, privateness, and aesthetic emphasis – but it is in modern critical reception that these qualities are overwhelmingly stressed. When I use the term 'Romantic poets' or 'Romanticism', I am referring both to an element within male poetry of the late eighteenth and early nineteenth centuries, rarely found in female writing, and to the construction that has been made from this element by later literary criticism.

The extreme value placed on Romantic poetry is allied to a downgrading of women's prosaic activity during this period. A professor of romanticism from Princeton recently began a lecture in Cambridge University on the early nineteenth century by stating that the spirit of the age was Romanticism; he went on to describe the transcendental male poets as the great peaks of literature, while Jane Austen and Maria Edgeworth were relegated to the foothills.

Women's choice of prose is seen, if at all, as a necessity, not a choice influenced by the moment and its polarities. Yet, for women in the later 1790s, reacting against their debasement by the sentimental myth and increasingly confident of their literary position, fiction seemed a way of inserting their works into culture as allegorical tales, ethical stories and active political agents. It is, I think, the transition to this newer kind of didactic writing that is recorded in *The Wrongs of Woman*, which can be taken as a paradigm of the interrupted fiction of the final years of the eighteenth century – fiction which, in the more liberal women writers, became the equivalent of the popularizing political journalism of the late 1780s and early 1790s. The transformation, the awakening or birth of the male poet from the rationalist and sentimental (that is, communal and nostalgic) dream into concern for the individual, the self and the visionary, is often depicted in Romantic poetry; Keats's *The Fall of Hyperion*, for example, captures the difficult ugly process of change. The transformation of the woman writer is enacted to less aesthetic satisfaction in Wollsonecraft's unstable novel.

Romantic poetry is seen by nineteenth- and twentieth-century critics (and by the poets themselves in certain moods) as a timeless mode that penetrated the surface world of signs to catch eternal verities behind. In the large-scale aesthetic works that defined Romanticism, beauty becomes not a quotidian efflorescence but a form of cognition, non-rational and non-empirical, and the aesthetic pleasure it gives was for Coleridge the object of art, beyond surface, surface truth and ethical and political instruction. Describing a later version of Romanticism, Roland Barthes spoke of its 'violent drive towards autonomy' which 'destroys any ethical scope'.

In *The Defence of Poetry* Percy Bysshe Shelley eloquently separated poetry from mere prose story; the former was an echo not of the world but of eternal music, the song that is always flying away behind the words. 'There is this difference between a story and a poem', he averred,

> that a story is a catalogue of detached facts, which have no other bond of connexion than time, place, circumstance, cause and effect; the other is the creation of actions according to the unchangeable forms of human nature, as existing in the mind of the creator . . . . The one is partial, and applies only to a definite period of time, and a certain combination of events, which can never again recur; the other is universal . . . . The story of particular facts is as a mirror which obscures and distorts that which should be beautiful: Poetry is a mirror which makes beautiful that which is distorted.[4]

The Shelleyan vision of poetry, of 'radiant disclosures' in Wallace Stevens's words, is 'of an eternal vista' of a 'poet's world'. Even when the Romantic poet tells a sequential tale, he insists with Shelley in the preface to *The Revolt of Islam*, that the poem is 'narrative, not didactic', not a social story but a succession of pictures illustrating the individual mind. In part this prefatory statement expresses the need of a political poet to diffuse his inflammatory subject-matter, but it remains true that this downgrading of the explicitly didactic does occur and that it is far more common in male writers than in female ones of the period.

In this version, Romanticism becomes like rationalism in its assumption that its knowledge is truth, a truth that is instantaneous, without history, past or present. The poet shares in the high conception of poetry, for he is inspired and godlike. Although he often aims to express the concerns of the common man and although he sometimes fears with Shelley a subjection to history, he partakes also in the authority and creativity of God and he becomes one with the prophetic voice; no longer subject to mundane law, he is transformed into a legislator, however unacknowledged.

The images and identifications are masculine, and indeed Romanticisim, protean and plural though it may be as an 'ism', is, in many of its guises and receptions, a reassertion of masculinity. The cry for manliness, mastery and virility echoes through the manifestos of Schlegel and Goethe. Coleridge demands the penetrating and mastering in art and rails against the effete and the effeminate, while Wordsworth, wanting a language available to all classes, sounds 'man' and 'men' with cumulative force through his prefaces. The abstract catchwords of political philosophy and rationalism have, he asserted in book 12 of the 1805 *Prelude*, womanized the nation, 'effeminately' levelled down the truth to simple general notions. In many ways this is a reaction to the popularizing political writing of the early 1790s, following the publication of Burke's *Reflections on the Revolution in France* in 1790, which sentimentalized – some felt vulgarized – the political subject to such an extent that it allowed women and lower-class men into political commentary. Educated men such as Coleridge and Hazlitt were partly trying to reappropriate the political for authority and for a more elitist culture. My point however is that women were part of this writing as they could hardly be of the later more elitist sort and that the reaction was couched in gender terms.

The Romantic poet's world is infinite, eternal and one, and the one, like the one of matrimony, is male. In the poetry of Wordsworth, Coleridge, Keats and even of Blake and Shelley, the female enters not usually as creating subject but as the symbol of otherness and immanence by the side of male transcendence, as a component in metaphors of reconciliation and integration, as emanation, shadow, mirror and epipsyche. The sexual act that needs the female idea becomes natural, nympholeptic and cosmic, a reaction no doubt to the assertively masculine abstract godhead of Jehovah, but none the less still a deeply gendered formulation. Heavily influenced by the feminism of Wollstonecraft, his dead mother-in-law, Shelley had a complex and profound vision of society and gender; yet even he does not escape the polarities. In *The Revolt of Islam* (1818) his 'poet's politics . . . in a poet's world' is envisaged as an awakening of the female will, an understanding by woman of her intellectual capacities. The visionary moment occurs as the heroine Cythna is transformed into the female equivalent of Laon, Laone, a woman warrior who preaches 'equal laws and justice' (IV, xx) and who joins Laon in a cosmically significant sexual encounter. The encounter is, however, more like self-integration than an expression of relationship – in the orginal 1817 version the pair were brother and sister – and after all Laone is Laon with a feminine ending.

In *Prometheus Unbound* the central drama includes Asia as well as Prometheus, but she is associated with the suffering passive world, mediating but not embodying intellectual beauty. The vision of Act III, scene iv of universal harmony once mental and political tyranny is vanquished finds the new man decultured, without class, nation, government or religion. He is not, however, specifically without gender, which is left at last with the biologically immovable constraints of 'chance, death and mutability'.

Wollstonecraft was alrady dead when Shelley was putting his poetic political vision in bottles and balloons and trusting them to the elements for a reception. Yet her final novel is an early reaction in a differing genre and time to the rationalist hopes that she and Godwin did much to inspire in Shelley. In the preface to *The Wrongs of Woman* she insists that fiction *will* be didactic, teaching awareness. It will not be primarily sentimental self-expression and it will have nothing in common with the poetic and privileged statement of aesthetic, psychological and moral truth. For the novel suggests a new awareness, that the truth is historical and may be caught in the very story that Shelley despised. The eternal verities of *The Rights of Woman* give way, then, not to mythical visions but to stress on the quotidian, on causes and on changing oppression, and on a connection of sound and understanding denied in the Romantic songs of the lark, the nightingale and the solitary reaper. Wollstonecraft's new vision is not encapsulated in political discourse or in timeless poetry but in story, not a form of representation as much as a way of seeing and writing of events, of the wrongs of women or, using Godwin's title for his own political novel, of "Things As They Are". Through narrative Wollstonecraft anatomizes the process by which gender oppresses in a specific historical time; women are burdened with a mystification through which they must inevitably act in culture and society. The book concerns the wrongs rather than the rights of women, not atemporal woman but historical women.

Like the Romantic poets, then, Wollstonecraft seems to have reasserted gender, although to different effect. She insists on finding woman in time and in unstable events and in moving from *The Rights of Woman* not because it delivers a false ideal but because it fails to take the measure of the historical and cultural construction. The novel, the tale of what is, fostering awareness retreats from transcendental reason or imagination and takes the path of history. 'The public are entreated to bear in mind', wrote Jane Austen in the advertisement to *Northanger Abbey*, that the 'places, manners, books, and opinions' in this work are of 1803.

Imagination is a good, but it is not the higher truth; sexuality can be fulfilling but it is not cosmic love. Everything exists in a constructed culture that gives it meaning and limits. So Wollstonecraft, the radical, joins the conservative Jane Austen, the liberal Maria Edgeworth and the cautiously radical Charlotte Smith in insisting that the everyday world should be understood and judged. In their own contemporary terms, women writers became the political and ethical historians of the late 1790s and early 1800s, not the poets of the Romantic period and not the sexually mirroring storytellers of Sadian fantasy; with the aid of the novel they investigated conditions as they were, deflating mystery and 'mere abstractions'. Sometimes pessimistically and confusedly, like Wollstonecraft, sometimes with muted optimism, with irony or with evangelical severity, they insisted on the material reality which might be momentarily escaped but which could not be transcended. They reacted with male poets to the apparent failure and contradictions of the rationalist analysis but, because of the added mark of gender distinguishing only one of the two sexes in culture, they found it difficult to embrace in its stead a mode that avoided the everyday world in which women were expected to acknowledge that they existed, a mode that both marginalized and mythologized them.

Wollstonecraft's *Wrongs of Woman* as story points in many ways to its own historical significance, towards a dialectical vision with Romantic poetry, to the more accepting domestic realism of Jane Austen and the Victorian women novelists who, despite their different intentions and complicities, also declared their business with history: 'there is no private life which has not been determined by a wider public life' wrote George Eliot.[5] Certainly it points away from the assertion of any transcendental atemporal truth, any intellectual system that is not investigated and embedded in the history that nurtured it, and from any art without ethical designs. Perhaps the measure of Wollsonecraft's distance from our concept of Romanticism, from the present, and from present psychoanalysis in her ethical aims can be gauged from a passage in *An Historical and Moral View of the . . . French Revolution* (1794). Writing of the Greek myth which had already given rise to so much seemingly timeless classical tragedy and which would come to loom so large in twentieth-century systems, she commented: 'The sublime terror . . . may amuse, nay, delight; but whence comes the improvement? . . . What moral lesson, for example, can be drawn from the story of Oedipus . . .?' (p. 228).

7

Men in Feminist Criticism

Some commentators feel that the issue of men's relationship to feminism should be addressed and, with the publication of *Men in Feminism* edited by Alice Jardine and Paul Smith (1987), it is a subject insistently out in the open. In this chapter I will concentrate on this book and its controversies.

Men in Feminism has a miscellaneous, hasty quality, reprinting the by now famous discussions of the subject by Elaine Showalter and Stephen Heath and filling in with various reprints, responses and counter-responses. The effect of the multilogues is to suggest some wonderful self-contemplating conference to which the reader was not invited, but which she must try to reconstruct to make sense of the discussion, an academic house party serviced by an international traffic of theory. None the less, with all its irritating inwardness, its almost silencing self-awareness, it does make a case for the problematizing of the subject and my initial reaction, 'why a volume called *Men in Feminism?*' inevitably anticipated within the book, is more or less answered.

But I remain uneasy at the book's existence. I am pleading for a rescue of a female component in the culture of the past so that we can use the historical awareness to change the culture of the present; any suggestion of a quick switch is worrying. The question of men in feminism often seems to resolve itself either into an effort to make women into something else or into the issue of masculinity on the lines of the already interrogated femininity; the latter topic then suggests that feminism has had its place in the liberal sun and should move over to leave the victim's space for a greater (male) victim, the homosexual.

I will describe a little of the criticism that treats men in feminism, masculinity and homosexuality (trying to remember always that the vast majority of male critics have absolutely no interest in feminist criticism and have read neither women writers nor feminist critics). I will end by predictably reasserting my point: that it is not time to foreclose on feminism, despite the desire of some men and women to have done with the subject after a mere decade, or to move on from the investigation of women as physical entities, whether single parents, Freudian daughters, or professional writers.

Male critics

By the 1980s an encroachment of male theorists as well as male theories was sensed by feminists. Some fashionable male critics were managing to assume a feminist discourse and write on commonly feminist subjects as if they had no more implications than a change of clothes in a dressing room, to use the notorious simile. So arose the questions of whether there was a place for men in feminist criticism and whether it was feminist criticism when engaged in by men.

In his introductory work, *Feminist Literary Studies* (1984), K. K. Ruthven described himself as 'a pro-feminist male' who believed that feminism was not a faith to be fortified but a truth-claim to be investigated. Manfully he took on the issue of male feminism, noting the controversial nature of men's participation and the antagonism it aroused in many feminists. He could hardly have meant to dampen it when he pugnaciously argued against the notion that academic men who profess to take an interest in feminist criticism will blunt its radical cutting edge; in fact, he declared, all the historical movements of feminism have been heavily dependant on men to articulate their positions. In the past it was Engels and John Stuart Mill; in the present it is Foucault, Barthes, Derrida and Lacan.

Ruthven became even more provoking when, inveighing against what he called 'feminist terrorism', the female equivalent of machismo, he asserted that men might be more successful at feminist criticism than women because they were freer to express dissent from certain extreme positions – male objectivity? – consequently with men's help a 'much better case can be made out for feminism than many feminists have succeeded in making'. Feminist criticism was too important to be left in the hands of 'anti-intellectual feminists, whether vulgarians . . . or highbrows' (p. 9). Such complacent and authoritarian remarks are especially unfortunate since the book is, on the whole, a fair and lucid introduction – once the introduction to the author himself is past. At any rate it provides a good illustration of the thorny problems of male acts and attitudes.

The same may be said of Paul Smith's essay in *Men in Feminism*. This reiterates the need for men to unsettle and undermine the settling laws of feminist discourse and forestall the academic institutionalization of feminism. It makes the Ruthven stand more threatening; 'Men,' Smith writes, 'still constitute a shadowy unlegislatable area for feminist theory.' Insisting that this theory be situated within an 'array of poststructuralist discourses with which many of us are now perhaps over-familiar', he suggests a kind of temporal menace for feminism, doomed to or already overtaken by the same dreary fate: to bore everyone.

The Anglo-American intrusion

Perhaps this was inevitable. In 1978 Nina Auerbach wrote *Communities of Women*; in 1984 she followed it with an article, 'Why Communities of Women Aren't Enough' in which she remarked on the way early feminist criticism created men as mythic, dehumanizing entities, in whose looming forms the entire history of women's oppression was written. Such enormous projections prepared us either for revolution or for a new more insidious repression, rather like the early twentieth-century one so scathingly treated by Kate Millett in *Sexual Politics*. The invitation to resist such expectations was presumably irresistible – men, rather liking the idea of our enterprise, started dropping by.

In the States the film star Dustin Hoffmann became a woman in *Tootsie* and loudly celebrated the fact and himself; the film drew on the fashion for chic androgyny in the USA of the early 1980s. In criticism, Jonathan Culler, Wayne Booth, Terry Eagleton, Christopher Norris and J. Hillis Miller all 'dropped by', that is, they took up a sympathetic stance towards feminist criticism, although several like Norris and Eagleton tended in their work to ignore the actual feminist critics who had contributed to their invitation.

They arrived in several ways. Some looked at the writing of woman in culture; Robert Scholes, in *Semiotics and Interpretation* (1982), noted the repressive cultural codes of female sexuality within language. Others investigated criticism and critical readings with gender newly in mind; Wayne Booth in 'Freedom of Interpretation: Bakhtin and the

Challenge of Feminist Criticism' (1982) noted Bakhtin's failure to account for the sexual difference in his notions of heteroglossia, the many voices of a single user of language. Jonathan Culler in *On Deconstruction* (1982) considered reading as a woman and he made his woman progress from a belief in feminist experience through self-awareness to a transcendental state in which she comprehends categories of thought and becomes – a non-gendered deconstructionist.[1]

Perhaps the most bizarre arrival was Lawrence Lipking who came by way of the Woolfian fantasy of Shakespeare's sister in *A Room of One's Own*. In 'Aristotle's Sister' (1983) he imagined a sister for the philosopher who would be concerned with theory not theatre, penning not a woman's *Hamlet* but a feminine *Poetics*. This poetics, however, turns out to be a 'poetics of abandonment' in which the victimized voice of women is privileged as a sort of frisson for men. Women end up simply as an aspect – and that a traditional one – of male culture; the critical possibilities that are celebrated have little to do with women and their victimized position but much to do with men's conception of them. As Jane Marcus noted: 'Like the ubiquitous recreations of the androgyne in art (always a feminized male) in the 1890s in responses to the last wave of European feminism, this proposal extends the range of male cultural action into the female.'[2]

Rape and *Clarissa*

The prolific Terry Eagleton is polite about feminist criticism in his many assessments and popularizations of critical theory, and his politeness is uncommon enough among male critics to be both encouraging and welcome. But it comes with considerable condescension. In his study of Walter Benjamin (1981), he decided that feminist criticism was 'empirical, unsubtle and theoretically thin', a bit clinging in its relationship to Marxism and psychoanalysis, and downright scandalous in its separatist designs. In *The Rape of Clarissa* (1982) he took on a text about a woman; Richardson's *Clarissa* had been of much concern to feminist critics who had helped to recover it from the Leavisite dismissal. Unfortunately, although he came into the feminist space with knightly desires, he appeared not to have noticed the inhabitants: 'The wager of this book is that it is just possible that we

may now once again be able to read Samuel Richardson'. Well, we had
been reading him for several years already.[3] Along with the female
critics, the female writers of the time were ignored; Richardson's novels
became the source of sentimental fiction and all the scribbling women
of the 1730s and 1740s disappeared.

Eagleton argued that *Clarissa* dramatized the contradictions of
patriarchy, 'marooned between ... doctrine and experience, dominance and dissemination'. The heroine became a self-referential sign,
and her lengthy ritual of dying a deliberate disengagement from the
patriarchal and class society in which she was assaulted. Lovelace, who
had been a problem since Richardson found him seducing the reader,
had recently been admired as one of the first formalists. Eagleton
rightly reduced him to villainy, but in modern fashion by making him a
psychoanalytical case. The rape itself became Lovelace's desire for the
lost phallus, for proof of female castration and for writing, now
considered female.

It was *The Rape of Clarissa* that caused Elaine Showalter to label
Eagleton a critical transvestite. Indeed she associated him with Dustin
Hoffman. In 'Critical Cross-Dressing: Male Feminists and The
Woman of the Year' (1983) she took Eagleton to task for his borrowing
from the language of feminist criticism, borrowing that did not imply a
willingness to reflect on his own masculinity or an admission that
anything personal and equivocal was involved in the criticism. So, she
argued, a kind of phallic 'feminist' criticism was created that competed
with women's criticism rather than aiding it; the male critic aimed, as
Ruthven would later admit, to 'show the girls how to do it'. She ended
her essay with a fantasy of male appropriation of feminist phallic power
through the notorious trope of clothing: we are all at an academic
conference when a critic comes to the podium – 'He is forceful, he is
articulate; he is talking about Heidegger or Derrida or Lévi-Strauss or
Brecht. He is wearing a dress.'

We must, she warned, treat the seemingly kindly incursions of male
theoretical critics with suspicion, since the feminist method might be
lifted from its political and social context and since it was necessary
always to remember the different stake that men and women had in the
critique of phallocentrism. And in the end, what works had been
chosen by men who ventured into feminist criticism? Even though their
deconstruction proclaimed the death of the author and so made
authorial gender unimportant, these works were pretty exclusively

created by men. Signature, then, remained important and it was dangerous to deny it: 'Like other kinds of criticism, feminist criticism is both reading and writing, both the interpretation of a text and the independent production of meaning. It is through the autonomous act of writing, and the confrontation with the anxiety that it generates, that feminist critics have developed theories of women's writing, theories proved on our own pulses' (p. 147).[4]

When considering *The Rape of Clarissa* specifically, I would want to go further than Showalter in taking issue with some of the *readings*, even more than with the choice of text. For all its panoply of feminist sounds and its very real perceptions, Eagleton's interpretation of *Clarissa* has turned a physical and violent rape into a sign; rhetoric and stylishness obscure the female horror of rape, political and inscribed no doubt, as Eagleton argues, but also historical, specific, physical and female-endured. (In much the same way, many feminists fear men interveners will turn feminist criticism into a stylish modality.) Having finished Eagleton's book, I longed to return to the outrage of one of Richardson's first readers, his contemporary correspondent Lady Echlin. For her no such soothing manoeuvre was available; she found the rape so frightful in its reference to an experienced world of violence that she felt 'strangely agitated' and 'her heart fired with indignation at those passages so horribly shocking to humanity'; she then composed a new ending to innoculate herself against their power.

The danger of Eagleton's reading, clever and entertaining though it is, comes not from an appropriation of feminism but from its conversion of a feminist issue, rape, used for the title of the book and picturesquely depicted in the dancelike Fragonard painting on the cover, into a symbol and a sign. Lovelace tried something like this after the rape. Similar appropriations and transformations continue in modern, often male, writings on rape, in such works as *Rape* edited by Sylvana Tomaselli and Roy Porter (1986), a book purporting to treat the subject from the perspective of anthropology, law, history, biology, psychology, philosophy, feminism, art and popular culture. The aim is anti-political, to oppose the slogans and simplicities of Susan Brownmiller's *Against Our Will: Men, Women and Rape* (1975) which contended that 'All men are potential rapists'; here the subject will be treated academically ' from a number of different viewpoints . . . so that rape can be seen in the broadest perspective'. I would have expected feminism to inform all the approaches to such a subject and the victim's perspective to be paramount (though I take Norman Bryson's useful point in his essay on the visual arts, that attackers and victims are almost the least privileged to speak about rape, which therefore exists for us in highly refracted form – though the 'us' may be a bit troubling here). Like Eagleton's criticism, this book comes with a tasteful rape on the cover, muted in colour and focus.

Obviously there is no need to oppose entirely the academic study of sexual violence; Eve Kosofsky Sedgwick's *Between Men* (1985) has acutely commented on rape as more than a sign and symbol, while at the same time refusing to allow it to arrive in art as unmediated representation; she gives a warning both to simplifying women and to mystifying men: 'it is of serious political importance that our tools for examining the signifying relation be subtle and discriminate ones, and that our literary knowledge of the most crabbed or oblique paths of meaning not be oversimplified in the face of panic-inducing images of real violence, especially the violence of, around, and to sexuality' (pp. 10–11). And we cannot say that men should keep out of certain areas. But I am pointing to a tendency for male interest in women to centre on the subject of the sexual, on pornography and rape. Such interest may, though it need not, come close in effect to the rather titillating use of the female body for medical display in the nineteenth century. In the end, I suppose, I would rather see a book entitled, *What Is To Be Done About Violence Against Women?* (by Elizabeth Wilson, 1983) than one called *Rape from different perpectives*.

Perhaps we *do* need to hold onto Brownmiller's simplicity which, as Michelle Barrett has said in *Women's Oppression Today* (1980), may be resented by men but none the less 'contains an inescapable grain of truth'. 'For if sexual practice is the area in which systematic inequalities of power between men and women are played out, then all men are in the position to exercise this power (even if only by mild pressure rather than brutal coercion), whether or not they are inclined to do so' (p. 45). I suspect that part of the reason that such a subject as rape can become modish is precisely the process contained in Eagleton's treatment of Clarissa and in the notion in literary criticism of 'hermeneutical rape'; if the concept of rape is naturalized as interpretation, then the material reality, the physical violence, all but disappears.

The Showalter article on critical cross-dressing is reprinted in *Men in Feminism*, where it is answered by Eagleton, himself in turn answered by Showalter. The exchange is a paradigm of the breakdown of discourse between men and women, British and American.

Showalter had quarrelled with Eagleton because of his ignoring of female experience; Eagleton counters by ignoring this point and in his response substituting class for gender. He cites his own northern working-class Marxist past in which he was uneasy at the help of bourgeois southerners; ultimately he came to regard his own hostile knee-jerk response as sectarianism. The autobiographical story is meant to be parable for and parallel to feminist critics unwilling to receive help from men. The response angered Showalter who answered briefly and tartly that either he had not read her article or he had decided to change the grounds of discussion and she saw no point in continuing a 'one-sided dialog'.

As a reader of this exchange I am immediately struck by the national differences it suggests. The British concern, even obsession, with class allows the translation that Eagleton makes; it is even a compliment, for women are being equated with the most esteemed of marginal groups. But the American experience includes no possibility of this compliment; reformist feminism flourished in the USA by obscuring the question of class and it received very little help from Marxism. Hence the translation is annoying to an American feminist, doubly so to Showalter since it was Eagleton's first act of translation – the rape into Lovelace's desire for the lost phallus – that provided the initial irritation.

Man's woman

The translation of feminism and woman into something else, exemplified in Eagleton's response, was a frequent manoeuvre of male critics. The most insidious version was the seeming silencing of the feminist discourse and subject-matter altogether through a reinstating of 'the feminine' within language. This enterprise, deeply anti-feminist, advertised itself as serving not the traditional misogyny of masculinity and femininity on any socio-cultural level, but a new 'femininity', the feminine as a modality or apprehension, the feminine as writing by – more often than not – men. To see the origins of this appropriation, already discussed in part in the brief outline of French theory, it is

necessary to return to the philosophical underpinnings of deconstruction.

French philosophers, influenced by German thinkers such as Hegel
and Nietzsche, had postulated the end of history, that is, the end of the
notion of the free empirical and unified individual acting in history.
There are no eternal truths and humanism, articulating the notion of
the truly acting subject is then bankrupt. Instead, the subject is not
defined through identity, what it is and what it does, but through
difference, what it is not. The not-self is needed for the definition of the
self, non-meaning for meaning. If there is no unified humanistic
individual, then literature cannot be written by anyone and texts
simply become inhuman, unconstrained by any authorial authority.
The enunciation and the rhetoric, formal equivalences, become the
question, and the old-fashioned notion of a content of historical truth
needing interpretation is rendered absurd. It is language that explains
and gives meaning to history not the reverse.[5] It is from a context of
such ideas that Lacan can say that the unconscious is structured like a
language, that it can become the object of a structural analysis and that
language is a code anterior to the message, not simply a medium for a
message. Derridean deconstruction was similarly part of this nexus of
ideas.

Initially deconstruction seemed liberating to women involved in
feminism. In his earliest work, before about 1970, Derrida insisted on a
feminist awareness of sex in looking and reading. In later work,
however, he stressed what Alice Jardine has called deconstructive
genderization, writing as that place where male and female remain
undecidable. In this formulation, women turn from being readers and
critics defined as non-male and become instead 'Woman', that which
will not be pinned down as truth. In the end the Derridean route leads
to a denunciation of 'feminism' seen as phallogocentric, constructed
within the traditional culture of hierarchical binary opposites. What is
reinstated in place of this phallogocentric feminism is the idea of
woman as a deconstructive device, for 'Woman has no essence of her
very own'.

In Derrida's formulation, the sexes are not opposed and their
traditional opposition is denaturalized, made unfamiliar, so that they
may be rendered equivalent. The questions to ask are then precisely *not*
those of feminist criticism, caught firmly in old-fashioned metaphysics
– how women may become subjects in their own right, for example,

how they might write at all, how they might write outside the patterns of patriarchal culture – since such questions are asked entirely within the phallogocentric world that should be opposed; feminism in this view becomes nothing but the operation of women who aspire to be like men.

'Woman' is then what is not feminist and the question becomes one of style not content. The feminine or 'the name of woman' is a kind of pre-logical destabilizing of texts, a writing which subverts logic and the traditional history of binary metaphysics. The texts Derrida chooses are on the whole by men and in them, as Alice Jardine has pointed out, woman is somehow what cries out to man, what puts him into question. The woman is that which refuses to name and do violence through naming. So, 'if naming is always violence, is the process of being un-named through a re-naming-in-parts any less violent? – even when born within a nonviolent, even at times feminist gesture?' (*Gynesis*, p.183). In Derrida the body image with which women have been saddled in traditional culture begins a strange disintegration into 'labyrinths of female voices, hymens, veils, vaginas, *tocseins*, traces, and texts. And it is from within those labyrinths that Derrida pulls on the feminine thread, unraveling the fabric of Western thought'. It is all very complicated, metaphoric, excited and exciting, but, like Lacan's formulation, it can be 'deconstructed' into some pretty traditional, predictable and libertine notions.

An interesting comparison can be made between the effect of this 'feminine' vocabulary on male and female critics. It is, for example, discussed in *Marxism and Deconstruction* (1982) by Michael Ryan who sees it somewhat unproblematically as designed to trouble the metaphorical assumptions about phallogocentric thinking and utopianly to point towards a new style based on difference and openness. And deconstruction must be good for women generally since women are naturally decentered. Christopher Norris in *Deconstruction: Theory and Practice* (1982) is more defensive: 'Of course there is nothing self-evident about Derrida's curious equation between woman, sexuality, and the swerve from logic into figurative language. What he is out to convey is the effect of a reading which "perversely" cuts across the normal conventions of relevance and hermeneutic tact' (p. 72). Women have not only become 'woman', but they have (re)acquired associations with the curious, the perverse and the tactless.

Female critics have responded rather differently. In 'Displacement and the Discourse of Woman' (1983) Gayatri Chakravorty Spivak, translator and in many ways apologist for the early Derrida, worries about the discourse of such men settling on the metaphor of woman. She sees it as harking back to that tradition which always made of women a generalized woman. Deconstruction objectifies woman, and Derrida is able to 'problematize but not fully disown his status as subject' (p. 173). In a recent talk, she accepted the epistemological usefulness of the Derridean idea of woman as the non-truth of truth, but she also saw its masculinist limitations; the feminist project of antisexism could not be identical with the epistimic project and the only way forward was to act through 'active forgetfulness' of the theoretical lessons.[6]

As I have already suggested, Alice Jardine also has some problems with the Derridean imaging of woman, the feminine in writing, and she regards it as the source of some clearly recognizable images and destinies of women. She asks, 'Are we here only brushing up against a new version of an old male fantasy: that of escaping the laws of the fathers through the independent and at the same time dependent female? Are men projecting their own "divisions" onto their primordial interlocutors – women? Do they hope to find a way of depersonalizing sexual identity while maintaining the amorous relationship through women?' (p. 207).

In 1985 Elaine Showalter gave a paper in England at the Southampton Conference on Sexual Difference; it was entitled 'Shooting the Rapids: Feminist Criticism in the Mainstream' and it discussed the seeming approach of Derridean deconstruction to feminism. It came to the following pacific conclusion:

> There has been a critical consolidation in the 1980s . . . because poststructuralists, feminists, and Afro-American critics share the same enemies: the rightwing champions of a nostalgic humanism . . . who advocate a return to basics of the classics, and who blame what they call the crisis in the humanities on newfangled ideas or unruly minorities . . . .
> As Derrida himself has explained in an interview at Brown, the programmes of deconstruction and feminism, especially with regard to the institutions of academia, have been similar. Moreover, Derrida notes, 'the resistance to deconstruction is exactly the same as that resistance which is opposed to women's studies . . . there is always something sexual at stake in the resistance to deconstruction'.

I would like to add to this, that the new theoretical methods – post-structuralism, deconstruction, and psychoanalysis – should make an absolute difference (if one can still use this word in an unreconstructed way) to feminist criticism. Their emphasis on language is one that feminist criticism needed and still needs, and their insistence on problematizing all 'truth' is a salutary example if not an instruction to our criticism. But because we are all fighting the same enemies does not mean we are fighting the same fight. If feminists have much to lose from 'nostalgic humanism', they have as much to fear from 'sexualized' deconstruction which may indeed make of woman something intrinsic to the entire conceptual system but which also fails to read her texts or notice her corporeal presence in the present or the past. There is something sexual at stake, I would argue, when women's studies fights deconstruction as well as when both fight rightwing champions.

Masculinity

Women were always subordinated to the concept of masculinity, which necessarily placed femininity at the edge, as the other of its self-definition. As feminist studies have emphasized, masculinity with its remarkably enduring myths of power is as constructed and as unstable as femininity. Kate Millett said as much in *Sexual Politics*.

Much work inspired by feminist studies has been done in the area of masculinity. For example, Barbara Ehrenreich's *The Hearts of Men* (1983) analysed the medical, psychological and social discourses of masculinity in American culture since the 1950s and noticed the collapse of the male breadwinner ethic through the notion that the earning male was under improper stress. With this notion feminism colluded and women were urged out into the labour force in great numbers. But the relationship of men's to women's wealth and earning power remained stationary and the change resulted in a large group of 'new recruits to poverty': 'women who had been middle class until divorce . . . severed their claim on a man's wage' (p. 172). Joseph H. Pleck *The Myth of Masculinity* (1981) uncovered the assumptions in seemingly empirical and scientific studies of American men from the 1930s onwards; he argued that what he called the 'sex role identity paradigm' – that is, the hypothetical psychological structure by which it was thought that an individual validated or affirmed his or her sex – determined and skewed both social and psychological research in which extraordinary misogynist and homophobic beliefs passed for facts. When psychoanalysis crossed the Atlantic, it provided a conceptual framework that allowed an intellectualization of the culture's pre-existing notions of masculinity. Many of these notions may well be held simply because they justify a relative privilege and are widespread in the culture.

In Britain there was stress on the context of feminism for the study of masculinity. The Masculinity Group was created at the intersection of feminism and socialism in response to the Left's refusal to rate gender with class in its analysis; using the techniques of feminism, it published several short papers in *Literature Teaching Politics* (1985) which argued for seeing masculinity not as an essentialist monolith but as heterogeneous, contradictory, social and historical, defined through its relationships to femininity, class, race and age. Peter Middleton, to take only one of the authors of the volume, looked at how masculinity was represented in a text of Wittgenstein noting the gendered subtext which sees philosophy as a struggle by masculine intelligence against the feminine bewitchment of language. Studying recent rewritings of history and noting the American obsession in television with law enforcement stories, Andrew Ross in 'Masculinity and *Miami Vice*: Selling In' (1986), considered the way male institutional authority reconstructed its credibility from the vacuum created by the Vietnam War.

For feminist criticism itself, the most useful development in the study of masculinity was a predominantly British stress on self-consciousness, of the sort revealed in Andrew Tolson's brief work, *The Limits of Masculinity* (1977), which placed its investigation of the prestige of masculinity in our culture within the framework of a feminism that had inspired him to a troubled awareness of himself as a man. Stephen Heath has, perhaps, taken this self-conciousness furthest. In 'Difference' (1978/9), he did what feminist critics have many times asked men to do, situate themselves as men not transvestites. But, since in the contest of American socio-historical and French psychoanalytical modes, with some protestation he sided with the French, the men and women he worried over were already somewhat rarified and over-determined beings.[8] *The Sexual Fix* followed in 1982 focussing on the construction of sexuality by the medical men of the nineteenth and early twentieth centuries, Charcot, Freud, Krafft-Ebing and Havelock Ellis. With this subject too there could be an avoidance of women, but a fascination with woman, the male mediation of woman, and female sexuality. Inevitably Heath's discussion raises the question of the voyeurism, even the pornography of the medical men – and indeed of the critic urged into quotation.

Of much of this Stephen Heath was aware and it was his awareness that made a later article, 'Male Feminism' (1984), alternately tortuous and refreshing: 'Is it possible to wonder whether there is not in male feminism, men's relation to feminism, always potentially a pornographical effect?' Although there is a whiff of narcissism and posturing in this article, there is much good sense too, for Heath noted that, while feminism must change men, women, still caught within the framework of domination and appropriation, remained the subjects of feminism: 'I have to realize – and this is an effort not a platitude – that I am not where they are and that I cannot pretend to be (though men do, colonizing, as they always have done), which is the impossibility of my, men's, relation' (p. 1). Women are not feminists by virtue of the fact that they are women but they become so by struggle and commitment; they negotiate between lived experience and feminism, awareness and knowledge.

> For a man the negotiation is blocked, doubly contradictory: his experience is her oppression, and at the end of whatever negotiation he might make he can always also confront the fact that feminism starts from there. To refuse the confrontation, to ignore, repress, forget, slide over, project onto 'other men' that fact, is for a man to refuse feminism, not to listen to what it says to him as a man, imagining to his satisfaction a possible relation instead of the difficult, contradictory, self-critical, painful, impossible one that men must, for now, really live' (p. 2).

Heath's article has been reworked and reprinted in *Men in Feminism* and, like Showalter's piece, has provoked response and counter-response. Attitudes tended to divide along gender lines. While women seemed to welcome his Irigarayan stance of admiration, men like Paul Smith saw this stance as sycophantic, almost 'another endorsement of fetishism' (a term of abuse in this sort of exchange rather like 'essentialism in the feminism of yesteryear). Probably there is something 'fetishizing' in the stance but the strength of the position, self-conscious and self-regarding though it may seem, is that it does not take away the political from feminism or, in the end, feminism from women.

Male homosexuality

One essay in *Men in Feminism*, situated in the lonely place of women in so many male anthologies or of feminism in anthologies of critical theory, is entitled 'Outlaws: Gay Men in Feminism'. It is here where feminist and gay studies meet, where misogyny or homophobia is the subject, that there is potentially most tension between feminist critics and men.

First, the feminist discussion of male homosexuality. In part it follows the rather dubious claims of Foucault that homosexuality as a cultural idea was invented quite recently, in the nineteenth century. Before that it was a type of now approved, now unapproved behaviour that anyone might fall into. It is, therefore, in its cultural construction distinct from the construction of woman. As a topic it grows in importance along with men's genderizing, as the sexual moves for its regulation from the religious to the secular – to the state, science and medicine. The compulsory nature of heterosexuality increases, as does the masquerading of homosexual or homosocial desire as heterosexual desire. Freud found society based on male bonding. Women disturb this repressed bond which reasserts itself in misogyny.

Irigaray discerns a kind of sublimated homosexuality in many of our cultural institutions, even in those which, like marriage, seem to inscribe heterosexuality. In phallic sexual theory, traditional heterosexuality simply becomes a mediation of homosexuality, a veiled homosexuality, defined here as the sexuality of the same, inscribing power between men and excluding the heterogeneous. So Kristeva uses 'homosexual' as a term of abuse for the 'feminist', the phallic woman entering the power structure of men. The ideological working of the paradigm is investigated by Eve Kosofsky Sedgwick in *Between Men* which describes the strategy by which homosocial desire – desire unexpressed in direct physical contact – is routed through women and heterosexual love. In such texts as Shakespeare's Sonnets, Wycherley's Restoration comedy *The Country Wife*, and Sterne's *A Sentimental Journey*, male bonding reinforces masculinity at the expense of the feminine. Women become the ultimate victims of the contradictions in a gender system that regulates men.

The oppression of women and homosexual men has been similar in several obvious physical and socio-historical ways; for every clitoridectomy for female desire, there has been a castration for homosexuality.[9]

A critique of the masculinist norms of the culture in which women and gays both suffer must reinforce the feminist assault on the hierarchical binary oppositons. So a gay writer like Jonathan Dollimore usefully reinforces a feminist point in his article 'Homophobia and Sexual Difference' (1986), that absolute difference is only ever in differential relations and that a difference is also a dependence.

But there are problems with the seeming alliance of subjects and Subjects – an alliance which on the whole gay men have not shown themselves especially eager to enter. In his *The Limits of Masculinity* Tolson argued that, ultimately, the masculine consciousness raising in which he was involved differed from the feminist version because masculinity was, after all, dominant in our society. It was therefore absurd to share vicariously the excitement of the victim. More recently, however, there has been some contesting among gays and women about who in fact is on the very bottom, or to put it in a contrasting way, a fight to 'annexe the high ground of the "victim" position'.[10] In this fight over who owns the margins or the height of abasement, it becomes a question of what opposes the masculine, feminine or homosexual.

The point was implied in the rather acrimonious *Sexual Difference Conference* in Southampton in 1985, which polarized gay men and feminists, some of whom saw this new formulation as an effort to switch attention from women before the analysis had been finished and before the feminist fight had been won. Simon Watney in his paper sounded distinctly hostile to political feminism which he reduced simply to a demand for a feminizing of men and a masculinizing of women, or a plea to shift the range of sexual identifications. He argued that feminism 'tends to pay attention to the cultural signs and economic sites of gendered inequalities to the neglect of actual sexual oppression'. I take it that 'neglect' is the important word here, but the sentence still appears odd to me, for, if the 'cultural signs and economic sites of gendered inequalities' are not sexual oppression, what is?

While we should all be aware that there are other oppressed groups and that many people fit into several at once, there does not seem much progress in valorizing gay in place of woman or of replacing one binary opposition with another, except that perhaps the process helps to destabilize all oppositions. Yet there is room for advance and many areas of possible co-operation. For example, in the critique of psychoanalysis which, in the Lacanian formulation, makes heterosexual masculinity almost synonymous with language itself. Gays have suffered from the constructions as much as women, and their analysis of and use of psychoanalytical methods can only help feminists get a perspective on this most dominating and privileged of contemporary myths.

The newer movements and the greater self-awareness of women and men such as Heath and Eagleton must be a good thing. The problematizing of masculinity from whatever source furthers feminist study and helps to gloss and revise cultural assumptions. But there is a danger that the study of men, masculinity or homophobia in literature will aim to supersede feminist criticism with its political aim and dimension, will cause not a swerve from and return to feminist issues and women's writings, but a straightforward march out of them, and will indicate that the time is ripe for leaving the old-fashioned margins of women's studies, and for entering into the mainstream, that 'male stream' that is always so copiously flowing through culture's centre.

The danger is greater because we live in a period of counter-reformation, conservative and liberal. Kate Millett saw a previous one occurring after the feminist reformation of suffrage; a similar one is discernible after Mary Wollstonecraft tried to appropriate the language of enlightenment reform for female social advancement and even tentatively for suffrage in the late eighteenth century. Counter-reformations emphasize gender and sexuality: Lawrence, Miller and Mailer or in the 1980s Roger Scruton and Ivan Illich who in *Gender* (1983) mystifies the power relations between the sexes into a folkish vernacular and enigmatic gender; predictably he soon arrives at a complementary masculinity and femininity, opposing the 'feminist dream of a genderless economy without compulsory sex roles' (p. 9).

To return to feminist criticism itself – that mode that must suffer the taunts of outmodishness. Women's voice from experience needs to remain at its base and, until men listen to it as well as imagining costumes and modalities for themselves, there cannot really be male feminism or men in feminism, simply men using feminism. One can, as Mary Jacobus has noted, be male or female to write feminist criticism, but no one can afford to become involved in its debate and practice 'without confronting the implication for their own critical position of that debate, that practice'. No one should enter it without knowing that he or she takes up a political position.

Conclusion

The strength of what I will now call the Anglo-American feminist approach has been its political implications, its refusal to separate the project of feminist criticism from the project of feminism, however defined, its willingness, in its hope for progress, to seem unimaginative and boring from a deconstructionist and psychoanalytical viewpoint. There has been much to criticize and uncover in Mary Wollstonecraft's writings and much to lament in the project of the enlightenment which she tried to foster and extend to women. Yet, however battered, deconstructed, and falsified, the enlightenment's individualistic bourgeois liberalism, its belief in rational advance and its aim of increasing freedom and equality through greater awareness of self and culture still form the ground of hope and of collective action.

The epistemological revolutions of our time have irrevocably made the Subject as well as our subject problematic. The unified speaking voice, like the great fraternal collectivity of enlightenment individuals, is a fiction. But so also is the dispersed subject of our own period. As the unified subject was the creation of an age of heroic capitalism when the individual had all to do and man was self-made (the problem of women's entry is amply suggested in Wollstonecraft's linguistic struggles), so the dispersed subject is part of the material reality of late capitalism, its flight from any notion of telos, its jaded contempt for anything but internal states and their narratives. The fragile self-conscious notion of some Subject need not be subjection when its historical construction is accepted.

There seems little use in questioning everything at every moment. Such questioning can only prevent activity and reduce the time for listening to answers, however partial and determined. It may be that for any activity a certain intellectual deceit is necessary, some pretence of an identity that is not entirely identical, an acceptance of some history even if its status as rhetorical story is suspected. As long as we know that we are ultimately not speaking for all and all time, that at every turn the various marks of race, age, class and so on should be noticed, and as long as we understand the ultimate impossibility of comprehending the past except through present structures, we may have to accept the useful fiction of 'women'; though we speak out of a cluster of conventions that have no necessary individuality or unity, we may have to hear a woman speaking as well as listening to speech 'in the feminine'.

Feminist literary history finds signature important. The woman who wrote is no doubt in the end unknowable, but, at some level or in some gap, trope or choice, she was working to be known . In her, history does become herstory and not simply hysteria, a generalized feminine predicament which can variously be expressed in man or woman. I agree with many critics of gynocritics that women cannot be separated out from the culture as a whole – in many ways they are caught in the same socio-cultural web as men. They probably cannot be formed into a separate tradition like Showalter's 'chain of writers' or Gilbert and Gubar's line of subversive voices. Yet I would like to argue for some affirmative action for them. To move too quickly into general study – or to add the 'best' to the established canon – is to risk entering the 'male stream' again and leaving the ratio of men to women where it always was.

The kind of literary history I am advocating finds genre important both because it makes discernible otherwise hidden ideological constraints and because it opens up the question of aesthetics. Demoted from its high romantic position as a universal truth, art has none the less an aesthetic of sorts, but it is worth considering what happens to the culturally constructed aesthetic when women artists are massively considered and what it implies for a political enterprise. Does it come only as icing on a cake that has been laboriously formed on other principles or does it have a basic substance of its own? Is it simply a pacific quality in the midst of conflicts, a pushing of traditional harmonies against the disruptive dissonances or a satisfying fulfilment of genre expectations?

Finally feminist literary history finds history necessary. There are external points of reference, however problematized, both in the past writer and in the critic herself who must know that she at least is in an historical world of historical things which constantly impact. Materiality cannot be always and entirely subsumed into the subject, history into psychoanalysis, epistemology into sexuality, or what Lacan mocked as the 'reality principle' of Freudian theory into the sign and the symbolic. But literary history need not take up a stance as the other of Theory; if theory has taught us anything it is that we are all theorized and that historical discourses of different kinds are never transcendental truths. Yet there is some truth beyond the text which gives an ultimate constraint on interpretation. It is only if there is no ultimate reality that interpretation or hermeneutics can become tyranny.

At the excited beginning of modern feminist criticism, relevance was haphazardly donated, conferred, discovered or uncovered in some writers and in some tropes or themes. Progress may now come from our growing surer of our history, refusing nothing as object of study, becoming less indulgent of the huge generalizations that seemed so relevant in the beginning, less concerned with immediate premature inclusiveness, less selfishly demanding of the past, less retrospectively arrogant and assured. Certainly there is much to be done both within our subject and outside; it will, for example, take a lot of careful work and some daring speculation to dent the extraordinary mythologies of Romanticism and Modernism or interrupt the great narrative of English literary history which has helped to create the critical terms with which women and women writers have been contemptuously judged. But, through the effort, women authors might be seen in connection with each other and with society; they might be understood as deeply disturbing to the aesthetic and cultural values that have kept them marginal to the creation of periods (and so to the creation of culture).

Feminist literary history is not a study of women as nature or of a natural woman, but of women intervening in culture, making culture, and being naturalized by culture in subtly different ways at different times; it is the study of the codes that intervene between subjectivity and history and help to fashion both. At the risk of sounding like a Victorian revivalist novelist, I believe that we should simply do more work of the archival and archaeological type on specific periods, while keeping in mind all the questions and possibilities of feminist criticism in its entirety.

As for the problem of male feminists, it is right as Stephen Heath suggests that men speak of their own masculinity in the light of feminism; they might also start reading women and recognizing feminist criticism. We would only be asking them to return the compliment of many centuries.

As historical critics we probably have to accept some chastisement from French theory while holding onto a belief in materialism. Feminist criticism may be another humanist gesture, another historical moment, anachronistic like history as Alice Jardine has expressed it, or even, as a recent appropriation of it has, rather obscurely, labelled it, the 'quantum physics of postmodernism' doomed to extinction in the electronic processing of image in the current mediascape.[1] But when history and literature have been problematized and deconstructed to the most rarified degree, a materialist something remains, if it is only a reiterated, variously articulated pain of difference and discrimination, oppression and repression. The woman writer of the past, present and foreseeable future is writing from a different space from men, however constructed and deconstructed her different circumstances and constraints. Although I do not believe there is a female identity that can somehow be known outside the patriarchy in which we and women of the past have all lived, I can accept a difference in male and female experience and I do not regard it as essentialist in any pejorative way to stress it.

It would be silly to elide or promote a premature synthesis of gynocritics and gynesis, but the two may quarrel creatively. If we can avoid the Big Dichotomies, we can take the historical method as basic and the other as occasional commentary, a critique not a complement. So works would become familiar, familial, and alien all at once, speaking to the present and out of the past. As readers we could read ourselves and then listen, so that we can sympathize with constraints that we might have outgrown and recognize in ourselves others that we did not know we had. We can avoid strangling meaning by pulling works too quickly from the past and by roping them round in predetermined patterns. What Germaine Greer wrote at the inception of *Tulsa Studies in Women's Literature* is still valid:

We have not reached the moment when we may generalize about women's work, because no generalization which is not based upon correct interpretation of individual cases can be valued. It is only by correct interpretation of individual cases that we can grasp what we have in common with the women who have gone our chosen way before us.'[2]

It is also necessary to grasp what we do not have in common, the different pressures and the alien comforts.

Notes

Introduction

1. Elaine Showalter, 'Women's Time, Women's Space: Writing the History of Feminist Criticism', *Tulsa Studies in Women's Literature*, 3, 1/2, Spring/Fall 1984.
2. Patricia Spacks, 'The Difference It Makes', *A Feminist Perspective in the Academy*, ed. Elizabeth Langland and Walter Grove (Chicago: University of Chicago Press, 1981), p. 14.
3. Jonathan Dollimore, 'Homophobia and Sexual Difference,' *Sexual Difference, The Oxford Literary Review*. 8, 1–2, 1986.
4. It is not only academics who assume the posture; the writer Micheline Wandor can be discovered with it when she declares herself marginal as a woman, a Jew, and a feminist in *Women's Writing: A Challenge to Theory*, ed. Moira Monteith (Brighton: Harvester, 1986).
5. K. K. Ruthven, *Feminist Literary Studies: An Introduction* (Cambridge: Cambridge University Press, 1984), p. 6.
6. In a recent article in *The Observer*, 14 June 1987, Claire Tomalin, literary editor of *The Sunday Times* from 1979 to 1986, takes issue with the thesis of a recent book, *Reviewing the Reviews*, that there is discrimination in the national press against women's writing and against women reviewers. Part of her refutation is a list of famous women reviewers; the first two names are Anita Brooker and Brigid Brophy.
7. I disagree entirely with the tone of another British woman who went to the States in the late 1960s, Sylvia Ann Hewlett in *A Lesser Life: The Myth of Women's Liberation* (1986), which blames the reformist feminist movement for forgetting the needs of mothers in its enthusiasm for legislating authority. Yet, beyond her immigrant's caricature of the culture of the period, it is possible to discern the very real misery of producing children and books at the same time, while denied even the maligned and traditional supports.

Chapter 1   Early Work

1. Toril Moi, 'Existentialism and Feminism: the Rhetoric of Biology in *The Second Sex*', *Sexual Difference, The Oxford Literary Review*, 8, 1–2, 1986, p. 95.
2. See Lillian S. Robinson, 'Who's Afraid of *A Room of One's Own?*', *Sex, Class and Culture* (1978; New York: Methuen, 1986), p. 146.
3. Some of the comment in *A Room of One's Own* was prompted by Woolf's observation of the poverty of women's colleges like 'Fernham' beside the affluence of men's establishments. Both sets of colleges exist in an outdated world of privilege, but it remains true that Newnham College, the women's college of Cambridge, is still relatively poor and Trinity College still rich.
4. In *Orlando* Woolf answered the massive conventional history of G. M. Trevelyan with the brief changeable story of a woman through the past; this story or history could only be told because the protagonist came from the upper classes.
5. Dorothy Richardson, 'Leadership in Marriage,' *The New Adelphi*, June–August 1929, p. 348.
6. For a short account of the emergence of feminist criticism from the 1960s civil rights movement and campus agitation over Vietnam, see Ellen Carol DuBois, Gail Paradise Kelly, Elizabeth Lapovsky Kennedy, Carolyn W. Korsmeyer, Lillian S. Robinson, eds, *Feminist Scholarship; Kindling in the Groves of Academe* (Urbana: Univ. of Illinois Press, 1985). Although published in 1985, this book in its interdisciplinary and collective nature catches the tones of the early period of feminist criticism when it was begun.
7. See Nina Baym, *Women's Fiction: A Guide to Novels by and about Women in America 1820–1870*. (Ithaca: Cornell University Press, 1978), and Jane Tompkins, 'Sentimental Power: *Uncle Tom's Cabin* and the Politics of Literary History', *Glyph*, 2, 1978.

Chapter 2   Consolidation and Reaction

1. See, for example, Cora Kaplan in *Sea Changes* (London: Verso, 1986), pp. 51–5.
2. On this problem of blindness and bias, see Margaret Homans, '"Her Very Own Howl": The Ambiguities of Representation in Recent Women's Fiction', *Signs*, Winter 1983.
3. It was not an easy time to edit a feminist journal, although several like *Women's Studies, Women & Literature* and *Feminist Studies* were flourishing during these years.

4. For an assessment of this new conservative phase, sometimes termed post-feminism or revisionist feminism, see Judith Stacey, 'The New Conservative Feminism,' *Feminist Studies*, 9, 3, Fall 1983.

5. Christopher Norris, *Deconstruction* (London: Methuen, 1982), p. 23.

6. Barbara Johnson, *The Critical Difference* (Baltimore: Johns Hopkins University Press, 1980), pp. 5 and 12.

7. The result of Showalter's attitudes in terms of critical commentary is heavy handed. Ann Douglas's overstated *Feminization of American Culture* (1978) is praised because it seems to deal with little studied women writers although its Puritan-admiring conclusions are clearly derivative of the established view that has long undervalued women's sentimental writing.

8. For an elaboration of this point, see Sydney Janet Kaplan's 'Varieties of Feminist Criticism', *Making A Difference*, ed. Gayle Greene and Coppélia Kahn (London: Methuen, 1985).

9. Adrienne Munich has also noted of Showalter's essay that the strictures on dealing with male material might seem a bizarre reinforcement of 'a primitive patriarchal taboo forbidding women to approach the sacred objects', 'Notorious Signs', *Making A Difference*, ed. Gayle Greene and Coppélia Kahn (London: Methuen, 1985), p. 243.

10. Maggie Humm has found the image running through the articles in Elizabeth Abel's *Writing and Sexual Difference* (1982), as well as through the work of Showalter, Annette Kolodny and Susan Gubar, 'Feminist Literary Criticism in America and England', *Women's Writing: A Challenge to Theory* ed. Moira Monteith (Brighton: Harvester, 1986), p. 104.

11. Elaine Showalter, 'Women's Time, Women's Space: Writing the History of Feminist Criticism', *Tulsa Studies in Women's Literature*, 3, 1/2, Spring/Fall 1984.

12. Lillian S. Robinson, 'Is There Class in This Text?', *Tulsa Studies in Women's Literature*, 5, 2, Fall 1986.

13. See Terry Eagleton's *Literary Theory: An Introduction*, (Oxford: Basil Blackwell, 1983), and Paul Lauter's 'Race and Gender in the Shaping of the American Literary Canon', *Feminist Studies* 9, 3, Fall 1983.

Chapter 3   French Theory

1. The strain of prophecy is apparent also in the nineteenth century and is described by Barbara Taylor in *Eve and the New Jerusalem* (London: Virago,1983).

2. Julia Kristeva, 'Stabat Mater', *The Female Body in Western Culture*, ed. Susan Rubin Suleiman (Cambridge, Mass.: Harvard University Press, 1986). In Kristeva's latest work on depression and melancholia the

privatization is expressed in individual psychoanalytical cases in which the author is involved as analyst. The generalization that French theoreticians were moving from public to private is very narrowly based; Monique Wittig, for example, moved towards greater insistence that there was indeed a material reality and that without the political dimension there was risk of a new mystification. See *Feminist Issues*, 1, Summer 1980.

3. Reprinted in *New French Feminisms*, ed. Elaine Marks and Isabelle de Courtivron (1980; Brighton: Harvester, 1981), p. 103.

4. This point was made by Margaret Whitford in 'Re-Reading Irigaray,' paper given in Cambridge, 1 May 1987.

5. K. K. Ruthven, *Feminist Literary Studies* (Cambridge: Cambridge University Press, 1984), pp. 100–1.

6. Julia Kristeva, 'Woman Can Never Be Defined' (1974), repr. in *New French Feminisms*, ed. Elaine Marks and Isabelle de Courtivron, p. 137.

7. Nancy. K. Miller, 'Emphasis Added: Plots and Plausibilities in Women's Fiction', *PMLA*, January 1981.

8. Marquis de Sade, *Juliette*, trans. Austryn Wainwright (New York: Grove Press, 1968), pp. 294, 492–3, 185.

Chapter 4   Confrontations

1. Geoffrey Hartman, 'A Short History of Practical Criticism,' *New Literary History*, 10, 1978–9, p. 501.

2. Another pervading trope, noted by Nancy K. Miller, is that of weaving used in literary criticism as a metaphor of femininity and connected to the metaphor of the text as texture and textile. It is deeply marked by Freud's account of women and weaving in his essay on 'Femininity.' See 'Arachnologies: The Woman, The Text, and the Critic,' *The Poetics of Gender*, ed. Nancy K. Miller (New York: Columbia University Press, 1986).

Chapter 5   Directions

1. See, for example, Jane Gallop 'Quand nos lèvres s'écrivent: Irigaray's Body Politic', *Romanic Review*, 74, 1983, p. 83.

2. Gaye Greene and Coppélia Kahn, eds. *Making A Difference* (London: Methuen, 1985), pp. 2–3; the quotation is from Louis Althusser, 'Ideology and State Apparatuses', *Lenin and Philosophy and Other Essays*, trans. Ben Brewster (New York: Monthly Review Press, 1971), p. 162.

3. In the Newton and Rosenfelt book some of the same essays appear as in Showalter's anthology. Sometimes this reappearance is due to their

representative nature – they may derive from a perspective less common in the context of feminist criticism, like the black and the lesbian, which anthologizers wish to include in a modest way. Sometimes these reappearing pieces seem to have achieved almost scriptural status as summations or historical interventions. This status is further conferred on them by yet another reappearance in a rather confusing volume (it is without index and dates) edited by Mary Eagleton, *Feminist Literary Theory: A Reader* (Oxford: Basil Blackwell, 1986), which takes excerpts from those texts rapidly achieving canonical status. In this area difficult theoreticians have a decided edge, for Kristeva, like no historical critic, proceeds towards a reader all of her own (ed. Toril Moi).

4. Lisa Jardine spoke of this sort of tendency in a paper given in Cambridge, 'The Politics of Impenetrability, or, Why Don't We Change the Subject?', 27 February 1987.

5. But some abuse and attempted coercion occasionally accompany the contribution. Alice Walker accused her former colleague, Patricia Spacks, of being racist because in *The Female Imagination* she did not construct theories of black experience. Cora Kaplan in 'Keeping the Color in *The Color Purple*' (1986) has taken us all to task for not appreciating Alice Walker's book, a great best-seller in the USA and Britain, and insists that, to get its intertextual resonances, we give it its cultural and political context of black women writers, southern white writers and misogynist black men. This insistence seems right to me, but I feel uneasy on being told that I *must* limit contexts. The novel may be a parable of black female subjectivity and may dig into Afro-American traditions, but those of us who also see it in the sentimental genre so often employed in nineteenth-century American women's literature, a genre that transmits nostalgic and reconciling visions of religious harmony, need not be mocked as admirers of an *Uncle Tom* made into a cliché of condescending racism. We are not necessarily looking askance at its enormous success if we consider this success as in part attached to its place in a cultural continuity.

6. Fredric Jameson, 'Reification and Utopia in Mass Culture', *Social Text*, 1, 1979.

7. Although I find the emphasis on pattern and myth rather constricting in Nina Auerbach's *Woman and the Demon: The Life of a Victorian Myth* (1982), the book does usefully force connections between elite and mass literature, insisting that Freud and Eliot exist in the same world as Stoker and du Maurier.

8. Marilyn L. Williamson, 'Toward a Feminist Literary History', *Signs*, Autumn 1984.

Chapter 6   Readings of Wollstonecraft

1. Showalter too in *The Female Malady* (1985; London: Virago, 1987) automatically moved from noting that Maria was in a madhouse, which in the book serves as a prison, to stating that the madwoman was an emblematic figure for Mary Wollstonecraft. Yet Maria was sane and it is we who make her into an emblem.
2. Theodor Adorno and Max Horkheimer, *Dialectic of Enlightenment* (1944), trans. John Cumming (London: Verso, 1986).
3. There are of course many excellent female poets of this period, for example Anna Laetitia Barbauld, Hannah More, Anna Seward, Charlotte Smith, Helen Maria Williams and Mary Robinson, but these are not labelled *Romantic* poets.
4. 'The Defence of Poetry', *Shelley's Poetry and Prose*, ed. Donald H. Reiman (New York: Norton, 1977). p. 485.
5. George Eliot. *Felix Holt* (Harmondsworth: Penguin, 1972), p. 129.

Chapter 7   Men in Feminist Criticism

1. In 'Reading Like a Man', *Men in Feminism*, ed. Alice Jardine and Paul Smith (New York: Methuen, 1987), Robert Scholes gives a lively and critical account of the Culler appropriation, while Nancy K. Miller wittily debunks Booth's embrace of the 'feminist challenge' in 'Rereading as a Woman: The Body in Practice', *The Female Body in Western Culture*, ed. Susan Rubin Suleiman (Cambridge, Mass.: Harvard University Press, 1986).
2. Jane Marcus, 'Still Practice, A/Wrested Alphabet'. While I agree with Marcus's comment here – and with her emphasis on the power of the constructions of male critics – I think that her article as a whole suggests another danger from this sort of male speculation, that it understandably provokes women into an essentialist response; Marcus continues her critique by positing another aesthetic, this time Penelope's, which grows out of a female culture defined as open, anti-hierarchical, and anti-theoretical, a poetics of commitment not a poetics of abandonment, connecting art with women's work in repetitive cooking, cleaning and weaving. I do not believe an aesthetic is to be found in abandonment or collective strength since neither image of womanhood seems universal and both are constructed out of opposition to the scheme of men.
3. The ignoring of a history of feminist criticism is by no means peculiar to male critics. I recently read an advertisement for the *Tulsa Studies in Women's Literature* which proudly asserted that the journal was 'the first

and only scholarly journal in the world devoted solely to women's literature'. *Women & Literature* was, however, being issued throughout the previous decade.

4.   Showalter's response in turn provoked a further response from Mary Jacobus in *Reading Woman*. Her objections pointed to some of the problems of male intervention and the purchase of women in their own criticism. Jacobus's prime objection was to Showalter's phrase 'theories proved on our own pulses', which she saw as essentialist and antagonistic to her own Lacanian notion, that textuality produced gender and equivocation. She regarded Showalter as closing the questions of gender that she had raised by 'invoking the experience of being biologically female'. In this premature closure, Showalter revealed to Jacobus a fear of dispersing gender identity; she also displayed a professional anxiety, presumably that men were muscling in on the only formerly undisputed area of literary criticism available to women. Disturbed by Showalter's final imaginative flight in the essay, when she fantasized the transvestite critic on the podium, she claimed that this rather girlish fantasy revealed 'the uneasy recognition that, when the text takes off its clothes, it is indeed disembodied, uncanny, silent. In other words, the very discontinuity of (female) body and (feminine) text is the scandal that experientially based theories of the woman reader displace onto the scandal of critical cross-dressing in the 1980s' (p. 13). Ultimately this is a restatement of the position articulated by French critics such as Kristeva (as well as a complex example of the body trope), and again I would take issue with the labelling of all experience, any impingement of the outside material world, as essentialist. An appeal to the nature of woman as something absolute, universal, transcendental and ahistorical does indeed seem somewhat foolish and for me it mars much American feminist criticism. But an appeal to an individual, located experience and awareness seems quite the reverse. I would then wish to criticize Showalter not for being too experiential and too historical here, but for being insufficiently so. There is a background and a context for the intervention of some men from particular institutional bases that could be described so as to illuminate both motive and effect; placing can be precise and sociologically shrewd as well as allusive and witty. Maggie Humm, for example, compares Richardson and his coterie of female admirers of whom much is made in the book, with Eagleton's coterie position in Oxford (*Feminist Criticism*, Brighton: Harvester, 1986, pp. 11–12). This is probably unfair, but it does suggest positions more likely to be held by men than women in our culture.

5.   For a full account of this philosophy, see Vincent Descombes, *Modern French Philosophy*, trans. L. Scott-Fox and J. M. Harding (Cambridge: Cambridge University Press, 1980).

6.   Gayatri Chakravorty Spivak, 'Feminism and Deconstruction Again', talk given in Cambridge, 3 July 1987.

7. As often with Alice Jardine the most interesting points occur either through self-conscious but still veiling metaphor or through (Derridean) questions that can in the end refuse accountability. None the less they seem to me to be the right questions.

8. Heath necessarily worries over the question of authority – insufficiently for Jane Gallop, however, who takes him thoroughly to task for the renewed authority of his stance, *Feminism and Psychoanalysis* (London: Macmillan, 1982), pp. 46–55.

9. For a discussion of this point see Vera Bullough and Bonnie Bullough, *Sin, Sickness and Sanity: A History of Sexual Attitudes* (New York: New American Library, 1977).

10. The phrase occurs in a response by Patrick Williams and Sara Mills to Jonathan Dollimore's paper in *Literature Teaching Politics*, 6, p. 70.

Conclusion

1. Quoted in Arthur Kroker and Donald Cook, *The Postmodern Scene. Excremental Culture and Hyper-Aesthetics* (Montreal: New World Perspectives, 1986), p. 22.

2. *Tulsa Studies in Women's Literature*, 1, Spring 1982.

Bibliography

Abel, Elizabeth, ed. *Writing and Sexual Difference*. Chicago: University of Chicago Press, 1982.

Adorno, Theodor and Max Horkheimer. *Dialectic of Enlightenment* (1944). Trans. John Cumming. London: Verso, 1986.

Althusser, Louis. 'Ideology and Ideological State Apparatuses', *Lenin and Philosophy and Other Essays*. Trans. Ben Brewster. New York: Monthly Review Press, 1971.

Auerbach, Nina. *Woman and the Demon: The Life of a Victorian Myth*. Cambridge, Mass.: Harvard University Press,1982.

———'Why Communities of Women Aren't Enough', *Tulsa Studies in Women's Literature*, 3,1/2, Spring/Fall, 1984.

Barrett, Michelle. *Women's Oppression Today: Problems in Marxist Feminist Analysis*. London: Verso, 1980.

———'Ideology and the Cultural Production of Gender' (1980). Repr. in *Feminist Criticism and Social Change*, ed. Judith Newton and Deborah Rosenfelt. London: Methuen. 1985.

Barthes, Roland. *Mythologies* (1957). Trans. Annette Lavers. London: Jonathan Cape, 1972.

———'The Death of the Author' (1968). In *Image/Text/Music*, trans. Stephen Heath. New York: Hill and Wang, 1974.

Batsleer, Tony Davies, O'Rourke, Rebecca, Weedon, Chris. *Rewriting English: Cultural Politics of Gender and Class*. London: Methuen, 1985.

Baym, Nina. *Woman's Fiction: A Guide to Novels by and about Women in America 1820–1870*. Ithaca: Cornell University Press, 1978.

———'The Madwoman and Her Languages: Why I Don't Do Feminist Literary Theory', *Tulsa Studies in Women's Literature*, 3, 1/2, Spring/Fall 1984.

Beauvoir, Simone de. *The Second Sex*. 1949, Trans. H. M. Parshley. Harmondsworth, Penguin, 1972.

Benstock, Shari. 'From the Editor's Perspective', *Tulsa Studies in Women's Literature* 5, 2, Fall 1986.

Bloom, Harold. *A Map of Misreading*. New York: Oxford University Press, 1975.

Booth, Wayne. 'Freedom of Interpretation: Bakhtin and the Challenge of Feminist Criticism', *Critical Inquiry*, 19, September 1982.

Bovenschen, Sylvia. 'Is There a Feminine Aesthetic?' *New German Critique*, 10, Winter 1977.

Brownmiller, Susan. *Against Our Will*. New York: Simon & Schuster, 1975.

Brunt, Rosalind, and Rowan, Caroline, eds *Feminism, Culture and Politics*. London: Lawrence and Wishart, 1982.

Bullough, Vera, and Bullough, Bonnie. *Sin, Sickness and Sanity: A History of Sexual Attitudes*. New York: New American Library, 1977.

Burgin, V., Donald, James, and Kaplan, Cora. *Formations of Fantasy*. London: Methuen, 1986.

Butler, Marilyn. *Jane Austen and the War of Ideas*. Oxford: Oxford University Press, 1975.

Chodorow, Nancy, *The Reproduction of Mothering: Psychoanalysis and the Sociology of Gender*. Berkeley: University of California Press, 1978.

———'Gender, Relation, and Difference in Psychoanalytic Perspective', *The Future of Difference*, ed. Hester Eisenstein and Alice Jardine. Boston: G. K. Hall, 1980.

Cixous, Hélène. 'The Laugh of the Medusa'. Trans. Keith Cohen and Paula Cohen. *Signs*, 1, 4, Summer 1976.

——— and Clement, Catherine. *The Newly Born Woman*. Trans. Betsy Wing. Manchester: Manchester University Press, 1986.

Culler, Jonathan. *On Deconstruction*. Ithaca: Cornell University Press, 1982.

Daly, Mary. *Beyond God the Father: Toward a Philosophy of Women's Liberation*. Boston: Beacon, 1973.

———*Gyn/Ecology: The Metaethics of Radical Feminism*. Boston: Beacon, 1978.

Derrida, Jacques. *Writing and Difference*. Trans. Alan Bass. London: Routledge & Kegan Paul, 1978.

Descombes, Vincent. *Modern French Philosophy*. Trans. L. Scott-Fox and J. M. Harding. Cambridge: Cambridge University Press, 1980.

Dinnerstein, Dorothy. *The Mermaid and the Minotaur: Sexual Arrangements and Human Malaise*. New York: Harper and Row, 1976.

Dollimore, Jonathan. 'Homophobia and Sexual Difference', *Sexual Difference*, *Oxford Literary Review*, 8, 1–2, 1986.

Douglas, Ann. *The Feminization of American Culture*. New York: Alfred A. Knopf, 1978.

DuBois, Ellen Carol, Kelly, Gail Paradise, Kennedy, Elizabeth Lapovsky, Korsmeyer, Carolyn W., Robinson, Lillian S., eds. *Feminist Scholarship: Kindling in the Groves of Academe*. Urbana: University of Illinois Press, 1985.

Eagleton, Mary, ed. *Feminist Literary Theory: A Reader*. Oxford: Basil Blackwell, 1986.

Eagleton, Terry. *William Benjamin or Towards a Revolutionary Criticism*. London: Verso, 1981.

————*The Rape of Clarissa*. Oxford: Basil Blackwell, 1982.

————*Literary Theory: An Introduction*. Oxford: Basil Blackwell, 1983.

Ehrenreich, Barbara. *The Hearts of Men: American Dreams and the Flight from Commitment*. London: Pluto Press, 1983.

Eisenstein, Hester, and Jardine, Alice, eds. *The Future of Difference*. Boston: G. K. Hall, 1980.

Ellmann Mary, *Thinking about Women*. New York: Harcourt, 1968.

Elshtain, Jean Bethke. *Public Man, Private Woman: Women in Social and Political Thought*. Oxford: Robertson, 1981.

Felman, Shoshana. 'To Open the Question', *Literature and Psychoanlaysis: The Question of Reading: Otherwise, Yale French Studies*, 55–6, 1977.

————'Rereading Femininity', *Yale French Studies*, 62, 1981.

Fetterley, Judith. *The Resisting Reader: A Feminist Approach to American Fiction*. Bloomington: Indiana University Press, 1978.

Finke, Laurie, 'The Rhetoric of Marginality: Why I Do Feminist Theory', *Tulsa Studies in Women's Literature*, 5, 2, Fall 1986.

Firestone, Shulamith. *The Dialectic of Sex*. New York: Bantam Books, 1971.

Fowler, Alastair. *Kinds of Literature*. Oxford: Clarendon Press, 1982.

Friedan, Betty. *The Feminine Mystique*. New York: Norton, 1963.

————*The Second Stage* (1981). London: Michael Joseph, 1982.

Freud, Sigmund. 'Femininity', *New Introductory Lectures on Psychoanalysis* (1933). Trans. James Strachey. New York: Norton, 1965.

Frye, Northrop. *Anatomy of Criticism*. Princeton: Princeton University Press, 1957.

Gallop, Jane. *Feminism and Psychoanalysis: The Daughter's Seduction*. London: Macmillan, 1982.

————'*Quand nos lèvres s'écrivent*: Irigaray's Body Politic', *Romanic Review*, 74, 1983.

Garner, Shirley Nelson, Kahane, Claire, and Sprengnether, Madelon, eds. *The (M)other Tongue: Essays in Feminist Psychoanalytic Interpretation*. Ithaca: Cornell University Press, 1985.

Gilbert, Sandra, M. and Gubar, Susan. *The Madwoman in the Attic*. New Haven: Yale University Press, 1979.

————eds. *The Norton Anthology of Literature by Women*. New York: Norton and Co., 1985.

————'Tradition and the Female Talent' (1984). Repr. in *The Poetics of Gender*, ed. Nancy K. Miller. New York: Columbia Unversity Press, 1986.

Greene, Gayle, and Kahn, Coppélia, eds. *Making a Difference: Feminist Literary Criticism*. London: Methuen, 1985.

Griffin, Susan. *Woman and Nature: The Roaring inside Her* (1978). London: The Women's Press, 1984.

Hartman, Geoffrey. *The Fate of Reading and Other Essays*. Chicago: University of Chicago Press, 1975.

———'A Short History of Practical Criticism', *New Literary History*, 10, 1978–9.

———*Criticism in the Wilderness*. New Haven: Yale University Press, 1980.

Heath, Stephen. *The Sexual Fix*. London: Macmillan, 1982.

———'Male Feminism' (1984). Repr. in *Men in Feminism*, ed. Alice Jardine and Paul Smith. New York: Methuen, 1987.

Heilbrun, Carolyn, 'Feminist Criticism: Bringing the Spirit back to English Studies' (1979). Repr. in *The New Feminist Criticism*, ed. Elaine Showalter. London: Virago, 1986.

Hewlett, Sylvia Ann. *A Lesser Life: The Myth of Women's Liberation*. London: Michael Joseph, 1987.

Homans, Margaret. '"Her Very Own Howl": The Ambiguities of Representation in Recent Women's Fiction', *Signs*, Winter, 1983.

———*Bearing the Word: Language and Female Experience in Nineteenth-Century Women's Writing*. Chicago: University of Chicago Press, 1986.

Humm, Maggie, *Feminist Criticism: Women as Contemporary Critic*. Brighton: Harvester, 1986.

———'Feminist Literary Criticism in America and England', *Women's Writing: A Challenge to Theory*, ed. Moira Monteith. Brighton: Harvester, 1986.

Irigaray, Luce. *Ce Sexe qui n'en est pas un*. Paris: Editions de Minuit, 1977.

———'And the One Doesn't Stir Without the Other'. Trans. Helene Vivienne Wenzel. *Signs*, 7, 1, Autumn 1981.

———*Speculum of the Other Woman*. (1974). Trans. Gillian G. Gill. Ithaca: Cornell University Press, 1985.

Jacobus, Mary, 'The Difference of View', *Women Writing and Writing about Women*, ed. Mary Jacobus. London: Croom Helm, 1979.

———*Reading Woman: Essays in Feminist Criticism*. New York: Columbia University Press, 1986.

Jameson, Fredric. 'Reification and Utopia in Mass Culture', *Social Text*, 1, 1979.

———*The Political Unconscious: Narrative as a Socially Symbolic Act*. Ithaca: Cornell University Press, 1981.

Jardine, Alice. 'Gynesis', *Diacritics*, Summer 1982.

———*Gynesis: Configurations of Woman and Modernity*. Ithaca: Cornell University Press, 1985.

———'Death Sentences: Writing Couples and Ideology', *The Female Body in Western Culture*, ed. Susan Rubin Suleiman. Cambridge, Mass.: Harvard University Press, 1986.

——— and Paul Smith, eds. *Men in Feminism*. New York: Methuen, 1987.

Jardine, Lisa. '"Girl Talk" (for Boys on the Left), or Marginalising Feminist Critical Praxis', *Sexual Difference, The Oxford Literary Review*, 1, 1–2, 1986.

Johnson, Barbara. *The Critical Difference*. Baltimore: Johns Hopkins University Press, 1980.

Jones, Ann Rosalind, 'Writing the Body: Towards an Understanding of l'Écriture féminine', *Feminist Studies*, 7, 2, 1981.

_____'Julia Kristeva on Femininity: The Limits of a Semiotic Politics', *Feminist Review*, 18, November 1984.

_____'Inscribing Femininity: French Theories of the Feminine', *Making A Difference*, ed. Gayle Greene and Coppélia Kahn. London: Methuen, 1985.

Kaplan, Cora, 'Pandora's Box: Subjectivity, Class and Sexuality in Socialist Feminist Criticism', *Making A Difference*, ed. Gayle Greene and Coppélia Kahn. London: Methuen, 1985.

_____'Keeping the Color in *The Color Purple*', *Sea Changes*. London: Verso, 1986.

_____*Sea Changes: Culture and Feminism*. London: Verso, 1986.

Kaplan. Sydney Janet. 'Varieties of Feminist Criticism', *Making A Difference*, ed. Gayle Greene and Coppélia Kahn. London: Methuen, 1985.

Kolodny, Annette. *The Lay of the Land: Metaphor as Experience and History in American Life and Letters*. Chapel Hill: University of North Carolina Press, 1975.

_____'Dancing Through the Minefield: Some Observations on the Theory, Practice, and Politics of a Feminist Literary Criticism', *Feminist Studies*, 6, 1, Spring 1980.

_____'A Map for Rereading: or, Gender and the Interpretation of Literary Texts', *New Literary History*, 11, 3, Spring 1980.

Kristeva, Julia. *Desire in Language: A Semiotic Approach to Literature and Art*. Trans. Thomas Gora, Alice Jardine and Leon S. Roudiez. New York: Columbia University Press, 1980.

_____*Revolution in Poetic Language* (1974). Trans. Margaret Waller. New York: Columbia University Press, 1984.

_____'Stabat Mater', *The Female Body in Western Culture*, ed. Susan Rubin Suleiman. Cambridge, Mass.: Harvard University Press, 1986.

_____'Woman can never be defined' (1974). Reprinted in *New French Feminisms*, ed. Elaine Marks and Isabelle de Courtivron, 1980.

Lacan, Jacques. *Écrits* (1966). Trans. Alan Sheridan. London: Tavistock Publishers, 1977.

Langland, Elizabeth, and Grove, Walter, eds. *A Feminist Perspective in the Academy*. Chicago: University of Chicago Press, 1981.

Lauter, Paul. 'Race and Gender in the Shaping of the American Literary Canon', *Feminist Studies*, 9, 3, Fall 1983.

Leavis, Q. D. *Fiction and the Reading Public*. London: Chatto and Windus, 1932.

Lipking, Lawrence. 'Aristotle's Sister: A Poetics of Abandonment'. *Critical Inquiry*, September 1983.

Literature Teaching Politics, 6, 1985.

Lundberg, Ferdinand, and Farnham, Marynia F. *Modern Woman: The Lost Sex*. New York: Harper and Brothers, 1947.

MacCormack, Carol P., and Strathern, Marilyn. eds. *Nature, Culture and Gender*. Cambridge: Cambridge University Press, 1980.

Marcus, Jane, 'Still Practice A/Wrested Alphabet: Toward a Feminist Aesthetic', *Tulsa Studies in Women's Literature*, 3, 1/2, Spring/Fall 1984.

Marks, Elaine, and Courtivron, Isabelle de, ed. *New French Feminisms* (1980). Brighton: Harvester, 1981.

Marx, Karl. *The German Ideology*, ed. S. Ryazanskaya. London: Lawrence and Wishart, 1965.

Marxist–Feminist Literature Collective, 'Women's Writing: *Jane Eyre, Shirley, Villette, Aurora Leigh, 1848: The Sociology of Literature*. University of Essex, 1978.

McGann, Jerome. *The Romantic Ideology: A Critical Investigation*. Chicago: University of Chicago Press, 1983.

McMillan, Carol. *Women, Reason and Nature*. Oxford: Basil Blackwell, 1982.

Miller, Nancy K., 'Emphasis Added: Plots and Plausibilities in Women's Fiction', *PMLA*, 96, 1, January 1981.

———'Arachnologies: The Woman, The Text, and the Critic', *The Poetics of Gender*. New York: Columbia University Press, 1906.

———'Rereading as a Woman: The Body in Practice' in *The Female Body in Western Culture*, ed. Susan Rubin Suleiman. Cambridge, Mass: Harvard University Press, 1986.

Millett, Kate. *Sexual Politics* (1970). New York: Avon Books, 1971.

Mitchell, Juliet, and Rose, Jacqueline, eds. *Feminine Sexuality: Jacques Lacan and the école freudienne*. New York: Norton, 1982.

Modleski, Tania. *Loving with a Vengeance: Mass-produced fantasies for women*. 1982; New York: Methuen, 1984.

Moers, Ellen. *Literary Women: The Great Writers*. New York: Doubleday & Co., 1976.

Moi, Toril. *Sexual/Textual Politics: Feminist Literary Theory*. London: Methuen, 1985.

———'Existentialism and Feminism: the Rhetoric of Biology in *The Second Sex*', *Sexual Difference, The Oxford Literary Review*, 8, 1–2, 1986.

———ed. *French Feminist Thought*. Oxford: Basil Blackwell, 1986.

———ed. *The Kristeva Reader*. Oxford: Basil Blackwell, 1986.

Monteith, Moira, ed. *Women's Writing: A Challenge to Theory*. Brighton: Harvester, 1986.

Munich, Adrienne, 'Notorious Signs, Feminist Criticism and Literary Tradition', *Making A Difference*, ed. Gayle Greene and Coppélia Kahn. London: Methuen, 1985.

Newton, Judith, and Rosenfelt, Deborah, eds. *Feminist Criticism and Social Change*. New York: Methuen, 1985.

Norris, Christopher. *Deconstruction: Theory and Practice*. London: Methuen, 1982.

Olsen, Tillie. *Silences* (1972). London: Virago, 1980.

Perry, Ruth. *The Celebrated Mary Astell*. Chicago: University of Chicago Press, 1986.

Pleck, Joseph H. *The Myth of Masculinity*. Cambridge, Mass.: MIT Press, 1981.

Pollak, Ellen. *The Poetics of Sexual Myth, Gender and Ideology in the Verse of Swift and Pope*. Chicago: University of Chicago Press, 1985.

Poovey, Mary. *The Proper Lady and the Woman Writer: Ideology as Style in the Works of Mary Wollstonecraft, Mary Shelley, and Jane Austen.* Chicago: University of Chicago Press, 1984.

Reviewing the Reviews: a woman's place on the book page. Written and edited by Women in Publishing. London: Journeyman, 1987.

Rich, Adrienne. *Of Woman Born: Motherhood as Experience and Institution.* New York: W. W. Norton, 1976.

———*On Lies, Secrets, and Silence: Selected Prose 1966–1978.* New York: W. W. Norton, 1979.

———'Power and Danger: Works of a Common Woman' (1977). Repr. in *On Lies, Secrets, and Silence.* New York: W. W. Norton, 1979.

———'Compulsory Heterosexuality and Lesbian Existence', *Signs*, 5, 4, 1980.

Richardson, Dorothy. 'Leadership in Marriage', *The New Adelphi*, June–August 1929.

Robinson, Lillian S. 'Is There Class in This Text?', *Tulsa Studies in Women's Literature*, 5, 2, Fall 1986.

———*Sex, Class, & Culture* (1978). New York: Methuen, 1986.

Ross, Andrew. 'Masculinity and *Miami Vice*: Selling In', *Oxford Literary Review*, 1–2, 1986.

Rule, Jane. *Lesbian Images* (1975). London: Pewter Davies, 1976.

Ruthven, K. K., *Feminist Literary Studies: An introduction.* Cambridge: Cambridge University Press, 1984.

Ryan, Michael. *Marxism and Deconstruction: A Critical Articulation.* Baltimore: Johns Hopkins University Press, 1982.

Sade, Marquis de. *Juliette.* Trans. Austryn Wainwright. New York: Grove Press, 1968.

Sayers, Janet. *Sexual Contradictions: Psychology, Psychoanalysis, and Feminism.* London: Tavistock Publications, 1986.

Scholes, Robert. *Semiotics and Interpretation.* New Haven: Yale University Press, 1982

———'Reading Like a Man'. *Men in Feminism*, ed. Alice Jardine and Paul Smith. New York: Methuen, 1987.

Sedgwick, Eve Kosofsky. *Between Men: English Literature and Male Homosocial Desire.* New York: Columbia University Press, 1985.

Selden, Raman. *A Reader's Guide to Contemporary Literary Theory.* Brighton: Harvester, 1985.

Shelley, Percy Bysshe. *Shelley's Poetry and Prose*, ed. Donald H. Reiman and Sharon B. Powers. New York: Norton, 1977.

Showalter, Elaine. *A Literature of Their Own: British Women Novelists from Brontë to Lessing.* Princeton: Princeton University Press, 1977.

———'Critical Cross-Dressing: Male Feminists and The Woman of the Year'. *Raritan*, Fall 1983.

———'Women's Time, Women's Space: Writing the History of Feminist Criticism', *Tulsa Studies in Women's Literature*, 3, 1/2, Spring/Fall 1984.

———'Feminist Criticism in the Wilderness' (1981). Repr. *The New Feminist Criticism*, ed. Elaine Showalter. London: Virago, 1986.

———ed. *The New Feminist Criticism: Essays on Women, literature and theory* (1985). London: Virago, 1986.

———'Shooting the Rapids: Feminist Criticism in the Mainstream', *Sexual Difference, Oxford Literary Review*, 8, 1–2, 1986.

———'Toward a Feminist Poetics' (1979). Repr. *The New Feminist Criticism*, ed. Elaine Showalter. London: Virago, 1986.

———*The Female Malady: Women, Madness and English Culture, 1830–1980* (1985). London: Virago, 1987.

Smith, Paul. 'Men in Feminism: Men and Feminist Theory', *Men in Feminism*, ed. Alice Jardine and Paul Smith. New York: Methuen, 1987.

Spacks, Patricia Meyer. *The Female Imagination*. New York. Alfred A. Knopf, 1975.

———*Imagining a Self*. Cambridge Mass.: Harvard University Press, 1976.

———'The Difference It Makes', *A Feminist Perspective in the Academy*, ed. Elizabeth Langland and Walter Grove. Chicago: University of Chicago Press, 1981.

Spivak, Gayatri Chakravorty, 'The Politics of Interpretation', *Critical Inquiry*, 9, 1, September 1982.

———'Displacement and the Discourse of Woman'. *Displacement: Derrida and After*, ed. Mark Krupnick. Bloomington: Indiana University Press, 1983.

Stacey, Judith. 'The New Conservative Feminism', *Feminist Studies*, 9, 3, Fall 1983.

Taylor, Helen, ed. *Literature Teaching Politics 1985*. Bristol Polytechnic, 1985.

Tolson, Andrew. *The Limits of Masculinity*. London: Tavistock Publications, 1977.

Tomaselli, Sylvana, and Porter, Roy, *Rape*. Oxford: Basil Blackwell, 1986.

Tompkins, Jane P. *Sensational Designs: The Cultural Work of American Fiction 1790–1866*. New York: Oxford University Press, 1985.

———'Sentimental Power: *Uncle Tom's Cabin* and the Politics of Literary History' (1978). Repr. *The New Feminist Criticism*, ed. Elaine Showalter. London: Virago, 1986.

Weeks, Jeffrey. *Sexuality and its Discontents: Meanings, Myths, and Modern Sexualities*. London: Routledge & Kegan Paul, 1985.

Williamson, Marilyn S. 'Toward a Feminist Literary History', *Signs*, Autumn 1984.

Wilson, Elizabeth, with Angela Weir. *Hidden Agendas: Theory, Politics, and Experience in the Women's Movement*. London: Tavistock, 1986.

Wollstonecraft, Mary. *A Vindication of the Rights of Men* (1790). Gainesville: Scholars' Facsimiles, 1959.

———*An Historical and Moral View of the Origin and Progress of the French Revolution* (1794). New York: Scholars' Facsimiles, 1975

_____*Mary, A Fiction* (1788) and *The Wrongs of Woman* (1798). London: Oxford University Press, 1976.

_____*A Vindication of the Rights of Woman* (1792). Harmondsworth, Penguin, 1985.

Woolf, Virginia. *A Room of One's Own* (1928). Harmondsworth: Penguin, 1973.

Zagarell, Sandra A. 'Conceptualizing Women's Literary History', *Tulsa Studies in Women's Literature*, 5, 2, Fall 1986.

Index

Adorno, Theodor 94
Adorno, Theodor and Horkheimer,
   Max: *Dialectic of Enlightenment*
   110–11
Althusser, Louis 85
anthologies 3, 47–50, 51, 90–3
Apollinaire, Guillaume 65
Ardener, Edwin and Shirley 43–4
Arnold, Matthew 27
Auerbach, Nina 9, 120
Austen, Jane 29, 97, 109, 112
   debt to predecessors 25, 29
   and the genre of her time 100–2,
   115–16
autobiographical intervention 7,
   105–7

Barrett, Michelle
   'Ideology and the cultureal
      production of gender' 88–9, 91
   Women's Oppression Today 124
Barthes, Roland 8, 65, 113, 119
   'The Death of the Author' 38
Bataille, Georges 65
Baym, Nina 24, 97
Beauvoir, Simone de: *The Second Sex*
   18–19
Beckford, William 104
Benstock, Shari 96–7
Bercovich, Sacvan 24
Big Dichotomies 79, 80, 138
Birmingham Centre for Cultural
   Studies 87, 94
black feminist writers 5, 37, 94, 144n

Blake, William 114
Bloom, Harold: *A Map of Misreading*
   24, 28, 35
Booth, Wayne: 'Freedom of
   Interpretation' 120–1
Brontë, Charlotte 47
   Jane Eyre 28, 107
   Villette 21–2, 36, 46–7
Brookner, Anita: 'Bonding against
   the Patriarchs' 10–11, 140n
Brophy, Brigid 11–12, 140n
Browning, Elizabeth Barrett:
   'Aurora Lee'
Brownmiller, Susan: *Against Our Will*
   123, 124
Brunton, Mary 25
Bryson, Norman 124
Burke, Edmund 106, 114
Burney, Fanny 29, 97, 101
   The Witlings 26
Butler, Marilyn: *Jane Austen and the
   War of Ideas* 29, 102

Carmichael, Stokeley 20
Carnochan, W. B. 12
Cecil, Lord David 8
Chodorow, Nancy 70, 72
   'Gender, Relation, and Difference
      in Psychological Perspective' 31
   The Reproduction of Mothering 31
Chopin, Kate 47, 51
Cixous, Hélène 51, 53–8, 61–3, 67,
   71, 78, 83, 111
   'The Laugh of the Medusa' 56–7

Clare, John 29
clothes as metaphor 45, 82–3, 119,
    122–3, 146n
Coleridge, S. T. 113, 114
Culler, Jonathan: *On Deconstruction*
    120, 121

Daly, Mary 38, 42, 62
    Beyond God the Father 32
    Gyn/Ecology 32
deconstruction 14–16, 38–40, 49,
    51–2, 56–68, 69–84, 126–9
Derrida, Jacques 17, 38–9, 52, 55–8,
    61, 73, 83, 119, 126–8
Dinesen, Isak: 'The Blank Page' 93
Dinnerstein, Dorothy: *The Mermaid
    and The Minotaur* 32
Dollimore, Jonathan: 'Homophobia
    and Sexual Difference' 6, 133
Doody, Margaret 3

Eagleton, Mary 36–7
Eagleton, Terry 14, 48, 89, 120, 134
    The Rape of Clarissa 121–5
Echlin, Lady 123
écriture feminine 53, 56, 67–8
Edgeworth, Maria 29, 101, 112, 116
Ehrenreich, Barbara: *The Hearts of
    Men* 129
Eliot, George 116
    The Mill on the Floss 66, 81–2
Ellmann, Mary: *Thinking about
    Women* 21, 25, 72
Elshtain, Jean Bethke: *Public Man,
    Private Woman* 37

Fanny Hill 10–11
Felman, Shoshana 3, 60
    'Rereading Femininity' 63–4
    'To Open the Question' 63
feminine writing (*écriture feminine*) 53,
    56, 67–8
feminist critique (Showalter) 41–4,
    66
Fern, Fanny 24
Fetterley, Judith: *The Resisting Reader*
    24

Fiedler, Leslie 24
Finke, Laurie: 'The Rhetoric of
    Marginality' 46
Firestone, Shulamith: *The Dialectic of
    Sex* 30, 38
Fish, Stanley 24
Foucault, Michel 82, 89, 95, 119,
    132
Fowler, Alastair: *Kinds of Literature*
    100
Frankfurt School 94
Freud, Sigmund 84, 93, 132, 143n
Freudian revisionism and feminist
    polemics 52–69, 69–84
Friedan, Betty 8
    The Feminist Mystique 20
    The Second Stage 37
Frye, Northrop: *Anatomy of Criticism*
    30
Furman, Nelly 92

Gallop, Jane 5, 8, 53
    Feminism and Psychoanalysis 45–6,
    64–5, 82–3, 147n
Gardiner, Judith Kegan 92
Genet, Jean 22
genre, study of 99–102
Gilbert, Sandra 3, 17, 28
Gilbert, Sandra and Gubar, Susan
    36–7, 47–8, 50
    The Madwoman in the Attic 28–30,
    33, 73–7, 100–2
    *Norton Anthology of Literature by
    Women* (eds) 3, 47–8, 93, 96–7
    'Tradition and the Female Talent'
    95, 96
Gilman, Charlotte Perkins: 'The
    Yellow Wallpaper' 24, 93
Godwin, William 104, 115
Goux, Jean-Joseph 95
Greene, Gayle and Kahn, Coppélia
    (eds): *Making a Difference* 87,
    91–3
Greer, Germaine 26, 138
    The Madwoman's Underclothes 28
Griffin, Susan 37, 38

Gubar, Susan 17
gynesis (Jardine) 78–81, 138
gynocritics (Showalter) 41–4, 66, 79,
   136

Hartman, Geoffrey 38, 80
   Criticism in the Wilderness 38–9,
   43–4
   The Fate of Reading and Other Essays
   38
Hays, Mary 107
Hazlitt, William 114
Heath, Stephen 118, 134
   'Difference' 130, 147n
   'Male Feminism' 131, 137
   The Sexual Fix 130–1
Heilbrun, Carolyn 9, 36
   'Brining the spirit back to English
   Studies' 27–8
Hoffman, Dustin 120
Homans, Margaret 3
   Bearing the Word 69–73, 75, 77
homosexuality, male, and feminist
   criticism 6, 118, 132–4
Humm, Maggie: *Feminist Criticism*
   31, 90, 146n

ideology, Marxist concept of 85–6
Illich, Ivan: *Gender* 134
Imlay, Gilbert 104
Inchbald, Elizabeth 29
Irigaray, Luce 17, 53–5, 58–64, 68,
   78, 80, 83, 132
   Ce sexe qui n'en est pas un 58–60
   Speculum of the Other Woman 54–5,
   58

Jacobus, Mary 1, 14, 17–18
   Reading Woman 59, 63, 65–6, 73,
   76–8, 81–3, 92, 98, 134, 146n
Jameson, Fredric 94
Jardine, Alice 1, 5, 8, 14
   'Death Sentences' 83
   'Gynesis' (1982) and *Gynesis*
   (1985) 73, 78–81, 83, 92, 95–8,
   126–8, 138, 146–7n

Jardine, Alice and Smith, Paul
   (eds): *Men in Feminism* 188–9,
   124
Jardine, Lisa: ' "Girl Talk" (for Boys
   on the Left)' 6
Johnson, Barbara 3, 39
Johnson, Samuel 35
Jones, Ann Rosalind
   'Julia Kristeva on Femininity' 68
   'Writing the Body' 67–8

Kahn, Coppélia, *see* Greene, Gayle
   and Kahn, Coppélia
Kaplan, Cora
   'Pandora's box' 87–9, 107–8
   Sea Changes 13
   'Wild Nights' 108–10
Kaplan, Sydney Janet 92
Keats, John 112, 114
Kolodny, Annette: *The Lay of the
   Land* 24
Kristeva, Julia 8, 17, 51, 53–6,
   60–8, 73–5, 78, 83, 132, 143n,
   146n
   'semiotic space' 53–4, 61, 68
   'Stabat Mater' 55
   'Woman Can Never be Defined'
   62

Lacan, Jacques 4, 17, 45–6, 52–4,
   57–65, 70, 77–8, 81, 84, 119,
   126–7, 133, 137
   Ecrits 52–3
Lauter, Paul 48
Lawrence, D. H. 22, 65, 134
Leavis, F. R. 8–9, 27, 75, 100, 111,
   121
Leavis, Q. D. 8–9
   Fiction and the Reading Public 94
lesbian feminist writers 5, 36–7, 94
Lipking, Lawrence: 'Aristotle's
   Sister' 121
Lukács, Georg 74
Lundberg, Ferdinand and F.
   Marynia: *Modern Woman* 10.
Macherey, Pierre 85

Mailer, Norman 65, 134
  The Prisoner of Sex 22
Man, Paul de 38
Marcus, Jane 36
Marcuse, Herbert 22
marginality, seductivity of 7–8,
  46–7, 60, 68, 140n
Marks, Elaine and Courtivron,
  Isabelle de (eds): *New French
  Feminisms* 51
Marx, Karl: *The German Ideology* 86
Marxism and British feminism 4,
  86–9
Marxist concept of ideology 85–6
Marxist Feminist Literary Collective
  87
masculinity, concept of 6, 118,
  129–31, 134
Masculinity Group 130
materialist feminism 90–1
McGann, Jerome: *The Romantic
  Ideology* 99
McMillan, Carol: *Women, Reason and
  Nature* 37–8
metaphoricity 44–7, 81–3, 143n
Middleton, Peter 130
Miller, Casey and Smith, Kate:
  Handbook of Non-Sexist Writing 11
Miller, Henry 22, 33, 134
Miller, J. Hillis 35, 38, 120
Miller, Nancy K. 9, 63
Millett, Kate 7, 8, 56
  Sexual Politics 2, 21–3, 25, 32–3,
  46, 65, 120, 129, 134
Modleski, Tania: *Loving with a
  Vengeance* 100
Moers, Ellen 9, 36, 37
  Literary Women 25–7, 33, 72
Moi, Toril 1, 8, 14, 18, 64
  Sexual/Textual Politics 57, 73–6, 78,
  83
Monteith, Moira and Rich,
  Adrienne (eds): *Women's Writing*
  90
Morris, Meaghan 79

Morrison, Toni 47

new historicist criticism 99
Newcastle, Duchess of 19
Newton, Judith and Rosenfelt,
  Deborah (eds): *Feminist Criticism
  and Social Change* 88, 90–1, 93,
  143–4n
nineteenth-century women novelists,
  critical emphasis on 26–7, 29,
  46–8, 69–71, 74, 97
Norris, Christopher 120
  Deconstruction: Theory and Practice
  127

Olsen, Tillie: *Silences* 21

Perry, Ruth: *The Celebrated Mary
  Astell* 97
Plath, Sylvia 51
Pleck, Joseph H.: *The Myth of
  Masculinity* 129–30
Pollak, Ellen: *The Poetics of Sexual
  Myth, Gender and Ideology* 69–70,
  72
Poovey, Mary: *The Proper Lady and
  the Woman Writer* 69–70, 72, 75,
  103
post-feminism 37–8
post-structuralism *see* deconstruction
psychoanalytical theory and
  criticism 4–6, 14–15, 51–68,
  69–84, 90

Radcliffe, Ann: *The Mysteries of
  Udolpho* 101
rape as feminist issue 121–5
Reich, Wilhelm 22
Rich, Adrienne 9, 14, 23, 37–8, 62
  'Compulsory Heterosexuality and
  Lesbian Existence' 36
  Of Woman Born 30–3, 42
  On Lies, Secrets, and Silence 31
  'Power and Danger' 62–3
Richardson, Dorothy: Leadership in
  Marriage' 20, 71
Richardson, Samuel 105

Clarissa 10, 121–2
Robinson, Lillian S.
'Is There Class in This Text?'
47–8
Sex, Class and Culture 35, 90
Romantic poetry 3, 71, 111–15
Ross, Andrew: 'Masculinity and
Miami Vice' 130
Rousseau, Jean-Jacques
Emile 107
La Nouvelle Héloïse 10
Rule, Jane: *Lesbian Images* 37
Ruthven, K. K. 122
Feminist Literary Studies 8, 60,
119–20
Ryan, Michael: *Marxism and
Deconstruction* 127

Sade, Marquis de: *Juliette* 53, 65
Scholes, Robert: *Semiotics and
Interpretation* 120
Scruton, Roger 134
Sedgwick, Eve Kosofsky: *Between
Men* 124, 132
semiotic space (Kristeva) 53–4, 61,
68
Shelley, Percy Bysshe 113–15
Shepherd, Simon 11
Showalter, Elaine 2, 3, 5, 9, 17, 47,
49–50, 72, 118
'Critical Cross-Dressing' 45,
122–3, 125, 146n
The Female Malady 42, 50, 145n
'Feminist Criticism in the
Wilderness' 43–6, 67
feminist critique/gynocritics 41–4,
66
A Literature of Their Own 26–7, 29,
36–7, 40, 42, 66, 73–5, 142n
and metaphoricity 44–6, 50,
122–3, 146n
New Feminist Criticism (ed.) 47,
49–50, 91, 144n
'Shooting the Rapids' 128
'Toward a Feminist Poetics' 40–2

'Women's Time, Women's Space'
45
Smith, Charlotte 101, 107, 116
Smith, Paul: 'Men in Feminism' 120,
131
Southcott, Joanna 55
Spacks, Patricia 8, 9, 37
'The Difference It Makes' 4–5
The Female Imagination 25, 144n
Imagining a Self 25
Spivak, Gayatri 8
'Displacement and the Discourse
of Women' 127–8
Stanton, Domna 9
Stevens, Wallace 113
Stimpson, Catherine 9, 69–71
Stowe, Harriet Beecher 24
Sunstein, Emily: *A Different Face* 106

Times Literary Supplement, The 8, 10–12
Todd, Janet
*A Dictionary of British and American
Women Writers 1660–1800* 9,
11–12
Sensibility 9–10, 12
Women's Friendship in Literature 9–11
Tolson, Andrew: *The Limits of
Masculinity* 130, 133
Tomalin, Claire 140n
Tomaselli, Sylvana and Porter, Roy:
Rape 123
Tompkins, Jane 24
Trilling, Lionel 24
Tulsa Studies in Women's Literature 145n

Victorian women writers, critical
emphasis on 26–7, 29, 46–8,
69–71, 74, 97

Walker, Alice: *Color Purple* 144n
Wandor, Micheline 140n
Watney, Simon 133
Watt, Ian 100
Williams, Helen Maria 9
Williamson, Marilyn L.: 'Towards a
Feminist Literary History' 98

Wilson, Elizabeth 124
Winters, Yvor 111
Wollstonecraft, Mary 9, 15, 29, 101,
    103–17, 134, 135
    *An Historical and Moral View of the
    . . . French Revolution* 116–17
    and history 110–11, 115–16
    imagination and sexuality in 104,
    108–9, 116
    and madness 105–7
    Mary, A Fiction 106, 108–9
    A Vindication of the Rights of Men
    103, 106

A Vindication of the Rights of Woman,
    100, 103–5, 108–11, 115
The Wrongs of Woman 104–9,
    111–12, 116
Women in Culture and Society 69–70, 72
Women & Literature 9, 145n
Woolf, Virginia 36, 72, 107
    A Room of One's Own 18–19, 21,
    27, 36, 74–5, 121, 141n
Wordsworth, William 114

Yearsley, Ann 29